COOKING WITH PARCHMENT PAPER

David DiResta

BRISTOL PUBLISHING ENTERPRISES
San Leandro, California

A Nitty Gritty® Cookbook

ISBN 1-55867-101-3

Cover design: Frank Paredes
Cover photography: John Benson
Food stylist: Suzanne Carreiro
Illustrator: James Balkovek

CONTENTS

Special thanks to Joanne Foran for her endless hours
of support, inspiration and dedication to keeping the project alive.

Many thanks to my mother and father
for their help and a lifetime of wonderful cooking.

To my brother, Michael, for providing and setting up the computer system.

To my brother, James, for eternal encouragement and confidence.

To Daniel, Jason, John Michael, Joseph, Katharine, Nathaniel and Paul
for sunshine, joy and dreams.

COOKING WITH PARCHMENT PAPER

WHY COOK WITH PARCHMENT PAPER?

From the popular *Seafood Wrapped In Parchment* to *Parchment-Wrapped Garlic Bread*, this book is an eclectic collection of easy, exciting and delicious recipes, all utilizing parchment paper to create special dishes. Widely used by professional bakers and chefs, this versatile cooking accessory is becoming a basic item in home kitchens.

Extensively known for its nonstick value in baking, parchment paper for cooking has assumed various modern uses for quick, healthy, no mess and low fat cooking.

Cooking in parchment greatly reduces the need for oils and fats, making it ideal for health-conscious cooks. Poaching seafood, for example, where fish and vegetables wrapped in parchment paper are lowered into seasoned boiling water, allows the foods to cook in their natural juices and creates an incredibly tender and delicious dish.

In addition to simply lining cookie sheets, parchment paper is used for creating parchment paper packets or as the French say, *en papillote* (pronounced *ON POPPY YOTE*), in which fish, poultry, meats, fruits and vegetables are tightly wrapped. The packets are placed in preheated ovens and foods cook in their own natural juices, creating a delicious meal. For an elegant, dramatic presentation, the packets are transferred to individual serving plates, which allows guests to cut open their own packets, releasing a delightful aromatic burst.

Parchment paper, at one time only available to professional chefs and bakers, can easily be purchased at gourmet shops and most supermarkets. Parchment is packaged in rolls or precut circles and rectangular pieces.

There are three methods for preparing en papillote or baked foods wrapped in an envelope of parchment. You can begin with a rectangular sheet of parchment paper, use a parchment circle or create a traditional parchment heart.

PARCHMENT HEART

To make a parchment heart, simply lay out an 18-x-15-inch sheet of parchment paper and fold it in half. It now measures 9 x 15 inches. With scissors, cut an imaginary line in the shape of a question mark. Unfold the heart and place the food on the bottom side of the sheet, next to the fold, leaving at least 1-inch borders along the three remaining sides. Follow the instructions in each recipe for the specific placement of ingredients. Fold the top half of the paper over the bottom and tightly seal the edges by overlapping small 1/4-inch folds along the sides. Fold the very tip a couple of times to create a tight seal and tuck it under the packet. Packets are placed on baking sheets and baked in a preheated oven. Parchment hearts create an interesting presentation at the table and are perfect for entertaining.

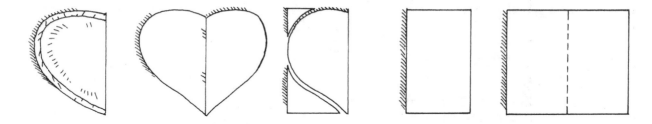

To open packets, either cut a large X across the top and pull back the four corners or slice open the three crimped sides and roll back the top section by folding it around your knife, using a fork as a guide. Slide the knife out when the top is completely rolled back.

RECTANGULAR OR CIRCULAR PACKETS

Although somewhat less dramatic but just as effective, rectangular and round sheets of parchment are prepared similarly to the hearts. Lay out a sheet of parchment, usually an 18-x-15-inch rectangle or a 15-inch parchment circle, and fold it in half. Follow the instructions in each recipe for the placement of ingredients. Close the packets and seal the edges of half circles with ¼-inch folds along the sides or a series of long thin folds.

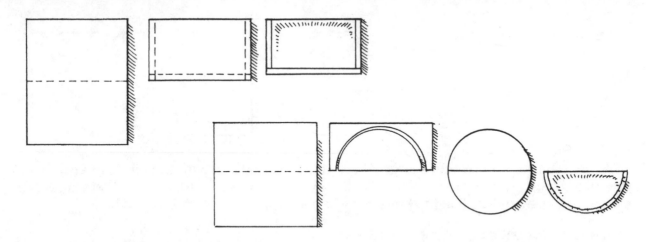

POACHING PACKET

To make a tightly folded parchment packet for poaching, lay out an 18-x-15-inch sheet of parchment and spread the ingredients in the center of the sheet. Bring the two long sides of the parchment together and make a ½-inch fold. Continue folding the paper onto itself until the packet is tight and the paper is against the food. Fold each end with a series of ½-inch folds until the ends are against the food. Secure the corners with paper clips. The packets are ready to be lowered into the simmering water.

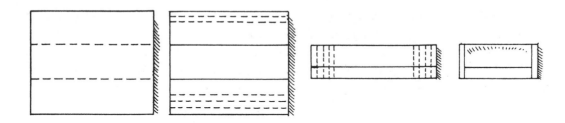

POACHING BAG

Parchment paper allows for a quick and healthy method for cooking fruits and vegetables. Place prepared fruit or vegetables in the center of a 15-x-15-inch sheet of parchment. Bring the four corners together, twist and tie to create a bag. Drop the bag into a pot of boiling water. Since parchment is insoluble in water, it never falls part. The cooked produce maintains its flavor and color and there's no added fat.

APPETIZER PACKET

The traditional Chinese way to cook an appetizer and keep it warm before serving is in an appetizer packet (see recipe on page 32). Lay out 4-inch square pieces of parchment paper at an angle. Place ingredients in the center of each paper. Fold up ½-inch of bottom corner. Fold entire bottom corner over ingredients and fold sides into center so they overlap. Fold packets in half, leaving top corner flap free to tuck in and secure.

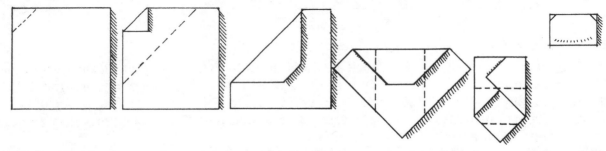

Nothing sticks to parchment paper. It transforms any pan surface to nonstick and it's insoluble in liquids. Casseroles lined with parchment paper not only cook perfectly but the cleanup is almost eliminated. Baked eggplant or roast chicken simply lift right out of the pan. There's absolutely no scraping, scouring or soaking. For baking, the foolproof dessert and cookie recipes are designed to cook on parchment paper and produce professional quality results. The grease-free parchment-covered baking sheets allow for reduced fat and burn-free baking. From the traditional *Anise Biscotti* to delicate *Ricotta Roll Ups,* perfectly baked goods slide right off the paper.

Once you have followed a few of these recipes you will have mastered the technique of cooking with parchment paper. Try experimenting by adapting your own recipes to parchment. Test kitchens emphasize wonderful cooking results, reduction in fats and elimination of messy cleanup. With parchment paper there are endless possibilities for baking, roasting or steaming.

OTHER CREATIVE IDEAS FOR PARCHMENT PAPER

Try parchment paper with your own recipes. To eliminate the grease in baking, insert precut parchment circles into **cake pans** or trace cake pans onto parchment and cut out desired shapes. Cakes lift effortlessly out of the pans. Use parchment for all your baking needs including jelly rolls, tube pans, pies, candy, meringues and fudge.

Famous retail bake shops use parchment paper to make perfectly browned **cookies** and brownies. When baking, you can reuse the same sheet of parchment eight to ten times without losing nonstick or insulating properties.

PASTRY DECORATING BAGS

Pastry decorating bags are easy to make with parchment paper. Simply cut a triangle from a sheet of parchment. Roll the ends on top of each other and twist the paper together to form a cone. Hold the seams together and twist the cone until the tip is completely tight. Fold the loose ends inside the cone to help maintain its shape. Cut ½-inch off the bottom of the bag and insert a pastry tip. Fill the bag with frosting to decorate your cakes and pastries. Another method, which takes a little practice, is to decorate without the pastry tip. Instead of cutting off ½-inch, just snip a little off at the point or cut at an angle to make fancy decorative lines.

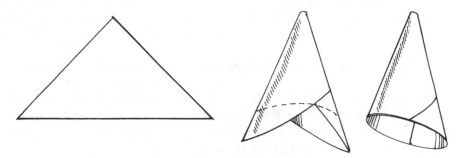

Parchment pastry bags are also great for dispensing soft butter and mashed potatoes or for filling cream puffs and cannolis. When you're finished, there's no cleanup; just throw away the disposable bag.

FRILLS

Meat and poultry frills are not only hard to find but they are also expensive. Making your own frills with parchment paper is simple and a fraction of the cost. Lay out a 15-x-5-inch sheet of parchment paper and fold it in half lengthwise. Roll the strip of parchment around your finger into a small tube. Hold the tube with your fingertips. With scissors, make a series of cuts on the folded side of the paper, ⅛-inch apart and 1½ inches deep into the tube. Place frills over the bones of a crown roast or poultry legs. Tie a small ½-inch-wide strip of parchment around the end of the frill to secure it in place.

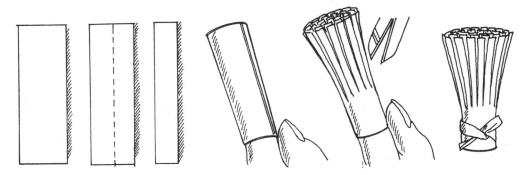

SOUFFLÉ COLLAR

Parchment paper reduces the difficulty associated with preparing and baking a soufflé. Place a parchment paper collar around the soufflé dish extending 4 inches above the sides, and secure it with a straight pin. As the soufflé rises, the parchment offers support and allows you to check whether or not it's completely cooked, by removing the collar and inspecting the soufflé. If the soufflé starts to fall, return the collar and continue baking.

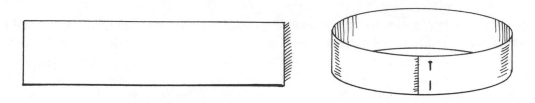

Parchment paper is also useful in **microwave ovens**. Place the paper over the food to prevent splatters and under the food to eliminate the mess.

Use parchment paper when **rolling out dough** to prevent it from sticking to the counter. Place the dough between two sheets of parchment or use a pastry board and one sheet of parchment. Roll out the dough with a rolling pin. The dough releases instantly and peels off the paper.

For **table decorations**, cut the parchment sheets into the shapes of leaves, flowers or hearts. Place them on a platter and cover with sliced cheese or appetizers at your next buffet for an interesting flair.

Try parchment when freezing cake covered with a delicate frosting. Did you ever notice how easily the lining peels off the frozen dessert cakes sold in supermarkets? That's parchment paper. Use parchment paper when **freezing foods** such as hamburgers and it allows patties to separate easily. It's also ideal for **transporting foods**. Caterers use it for **packaging** presliced cakes. Just separate the individual pieces with small sheets of parchment paper.

Parchment paper works wonders for **homemade pizza.** Sliding an uncooked pizza onto a hot pizza stone has always been a difficult task. Prepare the pizza on a sheet of parchment about 3 inches wider than the pizza, making it easy to lift. Place the uncooked pizza on the paper right on the pizza stone. The tiny pores in the paper allow the moisture from the dough to absorb into the stone, creating a perfect crispy crust. You get superb pizza every time and with parchment it never sticks to the stone.

Use parchment for **reheating** pizza or other baked products. If the pizza toppings are cooking more quickly than the crust, or toppings on tarts are browning excessively, cover with a sheet of parchment. The paper will peel off without disturbing the baked goods.

Use parchment paper in tomato-based or acidic recipes as a **replacement for aluminum foil**, which often reacts with the acids and flakes off tiny particles of metal, distorting the appearance and taste.

Whether you're rolling out a sticky pie crust or baking a delicate dessert, be prepared with a roll of parchment paper readily accessible. With today's increasingly busy schedules and limited amount of time to spend in the kitchen, parchment paper is a valuable accessory. Adapt it to your own cooking technique. I'm sure you'll discover many uses.

APPETIZERS

STUFFED CHERRY TOMATOES

Servings: 6

Serve these on your next buffet. They will be a sure hit.

18 cherry tomatoes
3 tbs. butter
1 medium onion, diced
2 garlic cloves, crushed

¼ cup minced fresh basil, or 1 tbs. dried
1 tsp. fresh thyme or ⅓ tsp. dried
½ cup breadcrumbs
2 tbs. grated Parmesan cheese

Cut tops off tomatoes and gently scoop out insides. Do not pierce sides. Turn tomatoes upside down and drain. Melt butter in a sauté pan and cook onions, garlic, basil and thyme for 3 minutes. Add breadcrumbs and sauté for 2 more minutes. Remove from heat and cool for 10 minutes. Add cheese and mix. Gently spoon stuffing into hollowed tomatoes. Lay out a 16-inch sheet of parchment paper and fold in half. Place parchment paper in a rectangular ovenproof serving dish and unfold. Arrange tomatoes in single layer on paper. Fold and tightly seal parchment paper. Bake in a preheated 350° oven for 15 minutes. Cut open paper. Serve hot or cold.

STUFFED MUSHROOMS
Servings: 8

For easy preparation, invest in a good mushroom brush. If you use water to clean the mushrooms, they will absorb more moisture.

2-3 lb. medium mushroom caps
½ cup butter
2 garlic cloves, crushed
1 medium onion, finely chopped

12 oz. fresh spinach, trimmed, coarsely chopped, or frozen, thawed
3 cups breadcrumbs
4 tbs. grated Parmesan cheese

Remove stems from mushrooms. Melt butter in a sauté pan over medium heat. Add garlic, onion and spinach; sauté for 3 minutes. Add breadcrumbs and sauté for another 3 minutes. Remove from heat and cool for 10 minutes. Add cheese and mix well. Stuff mushroom caps with mixture. Lay out a 16-inch sheet of parchment paper and fold. Place paper in a rectangular ovenproof baking dish and unfold. Arrange filled mushrooms on paper, fold and seal tightly. Bake in a preheated 350° oven for 20 minutes. Cut paper open and serve hot from paper-lined dish.

ROASTED GARLIC

Servings: 8-10

Roasting garlic mellows its pungency and lets you enjoy the sweeter flavor.

4 large garlic bulbs
2 tsp. olive oil
1 tbs. butter
1/4 tsp. dried basil
freshly ground pepper to taste

Cut 1/4-inch off tops of garlic bulbs. Remove loose outer leaves. Bulbs should remain intact. Lay out an 18-x-15-inch sheet of parchment paper and fold in half. Unfold sheet, brush inside of paper with oil and place 4 bulbs on one side of paper. Pour 1/4 tsp. oil over each bulb and dot with butter. Sprinkle with basil and ground pepper. Fold and seal edges tightly. Place on a baking sheet and bake for 1 hour at 300°. Cut open parchment paper and bake for additional 20 minutes. Separate cloves and squeeze garlic out. Serve warm as a spread for hot crusty bread rounds or crackers.

CHEDDAR-WRAPPED OLIVES
Yields: 36

This is quick and easy to prepare. Your guests will find these addictive.

¼ cup butter, softened
¾ cup shredded cheddar cheese
¼ cup shredded Monterey Jack cheese
1 cup flour
1 tsp. chopped fresh chives
2 tbs. water
3 dozen large pitted black olives

In a medium bowl, cream together butter and cheese. Blend flour into mixture and add chives. Starting with 1 tablespoon, add water as needed to form dough. Roll dough out into a thin sheet and cut into 2-x-3-inch pieces. Wrap each olive with a piece of dough. Place on a parchment-lined baking sheet and bake in a preheated 400° oven for 18 minutes. Serve warm.

MIXED CHEESE CRISPS

Servings: 6

Parchment paper makes it possible to combine a variety of cheeses to create an extraordinary blend. These have a crunchy texture, are spicy and excellent for buffets as an antipasto. You should serve them within an hour or two after preparing.

1 cup shredded mozzarella cheese
1 cup shredded sharp cheddar cheese
1 cup shredded Monterey Jack cheese

1 tsp. grated Parmesan cheese
½ tsp. dried red pepper flakes
½ tsp. dried jalapeño pepper flakes

Alternately sprinkle all ingredients onto two 18-x-12-inch parchment-lined baking sheets until they form a thin layer. Place in a preheated 375° oven for 14 minutes or until crisp. Remove from oven and cool. Peel cheese crisp off parchment. Break into small pieces and lay on paper towels to absorb excess oils. Serve with fresh fruits or crackers.

ROASTED PEPPERS WITH GARLIC
Servings: 4

This is a traditional Italian favorite that I acquired from my father. Roasting peppers in parchment eliminates the mess, reduces the cooking time and prepares the peppers perfectly.

4 large red bell peppers
3 garlic cloves, minced
1/2 cup extra virgin olive oil

Remove seeds from peppers and cut into quarters. Lay out two 18-x-15-inch sheets of parchment paper and fold in half. Unfold papers and place half of peppers on one side of each sheet. Fold and seal tightly. Place packets on a baking sheet in a preheated 450° oven for 30 minutes. Cut open parchment packets and cool for 30 minutes. Peel blistered skin off peppers. Cut into 1½-inch strips and combine with garlic and oil. Refrigerate for at least 2 hours. Serve cold.

SEAFOOD BAKE

Servings: 12-15

A seafood feast baked in parchment paper makes a unique presentation.

1 lb. clams in shells
1 lb. swordfish or halibut
2 cups fresh spinach, trimmed,
  stemmed
2 dozen large shrimp, shelled,
  deveined

4 tbs. lemon juice
1 garlic clove, minced
4 tbs. finely chopped fresh parsley
½ tsp. freshly ground pepper
¼ cup butter
10-12 lemon wedges

Scrub clams thoroughly under cold water with a stiff brush. Cut fish into pieces, approximately 2-x-2-inch squares. Lay out four 18-x-15-inch sheets of parchment paper and fold in half. Unfold papers and place equal amounts of spinach on one side of each sheet next to fold. Scatter ¼ of clams, fish and shrimp over each bed of spinach. Drizzle with lemon juice; sprinkle with garlic, parsley and pepper. Dot with butter. Fold and tightly seal each packet. Place packets on baking sheets and bake in a preheated 350° oven for 30 minutes. Transfer packets to serving platters. Cut open tops and serve with lemon wedges.

HERB GARLIC BREAD
Servings: 16

*This makes a great beginning. Serve with fresh green grapes and wine. Cut the recipe in half to prepare just one loaf. For variety, serve toast rounds or points with **Garlic Pepper Butter** from a chilled ramekin.*

2 loaves French or Italian bread
1/2 cup butter, softened
1 tsp. dried basil

2 garlic cloves, crushed
1/2 tsp. dried oregano
Garlic Pepper Butter, follows

Slice bread at an angle 3/4-inch deep at 1-inch intervals. Cream together butter, basil, garlic and oregano. Generously spread mixture between bread slices. Wrap each loaf tightly in a sheet of parchment paper. Place on a baking sheet or baking stone. Bake in a preheated 350° oven for 20 minutes. Serve warm.

GARLIC PEPPER BUTTER

1/2 cup butter, softened
2 garlic cloves, crushed

1/8 tsp. freshly ground pepper

Cream ingredients together in a small bowl.

MUSHROOMS AGLIOE OLIO

Servings: 4

Or call it mushrooms with garlic and oil. This is a classic, easy-to-prepare recipe with an intense aroma of garlic and stewed tomatoes.

24 mushroom caps
⅛ cup sherry
⅓ cup olive oil
½ cup chopped, stewed tomatoes with
 juice

2 garlic cloves, minced
½ tsp. dried basil
⅛ tsp. freshly ground pepper
2 tbs. grated Parmesan cheese

In a large bowl, combine mushrooms, sherry, oil, tomatoes, garlic, basil and pepper. Lay out an 18-x-15-inch sheet of parchment paper in a shallow ovenproof casserole. Carefully spoon mushroom mixture into center of paper. Quickly pull up corners of paper to form a bag. Secure with a metal wire or paper clip as on page 9. Bake in a preheated oven at 350° for 25 minutes. Pour into a large serving bowl or individual serving bowls. Sprinkle with Parmesan cheese and serve with fresh bread.

POACHED SCALLOPS
Servings: 2

The natural flavors of scallops are enhanced when they are prepared in paper-wrapped packets and cooked in boiling water.

½ lb. whole bay scallops, or sea
  scallops, cut into thirds
2 qt. water
1 onion, thinly sliced
1 bay leaf
2 whole cloves

1 tsp. vinegar
¼ cup shredded carrots
1 tbs. butter, thinly sliced
⅛ tsp. parsley
4 lemon wedges

Rinse scallops under cold water and pat dry. Bring water to a boil in a 3-quart sauté pan. Add onion, bay leaf, cloves and vinegar to water and simmer for 5 minutes. Lay out two 18-x-15-inch sheets of parchment paper and fold in half. Unfold paper and place half the carrots on top of each sheet next to fold. Place half the scallops on top of carrots. Do not let scallops overlap. Dot with thin slices of butter and season with parsley. Fold paper packets and secure wrap with paper clips for poaching. Lower packets into sauté pan and simmer for 8 minutes. Remove packets from pan and transfer to individual serving plates. Serve with lemon wedges.

SHRIMP AND SCALLOP PACKETS

Servings: 15

These can be prepared up to 2 hours before cooking.

1 lb. medium shrimp, shelled, deveined
1 lb. whole bay scallops, or sea scallops,
  cut into thirds
½ cup white wine
juice of 1 lemon

2 garlic cloves, minced
salt and pepper to taste
2 cups chopped fresh spinach, trimmed,
  stemmed
2 tsp. parsley

In a large bowl, combine shrimp, scallops, wine, lemon juice, garlic, salt and pepper. Mix and marinate for 20 minutes. Lay out fifteen 7½-x-8-inch sheets of parchment paper and fold in half. Unfold all sheets and place a small bed of spinach next to fold on one side of each sheet. Top spinach with a scoop of shrimp and scallop mixture. Each packet should contain 2 to 3 shrimp and scallops. Sprinkle with parsley. Fold and tightly seal each packet. Place packets on baking sheets and bake in a preheated 400° oven for 10 minutes. Transfer packets to a warm serving platter. Cut open and serve immediately.

BARBECUED SPARERIBS

Servings: 12-14

The parchment paper eliminates the usual mess.

6 lb. spareribs
1 cup dry sherry
1 cup honey
1 tsp. ginger
2½ tbs. brown sugar
1 tsp. garlic powder
4 tbs. minced onion
½ tsp. dry mustard

Cut ribs into individual pieces. In a large bowl, combine all ingredients except spareribs. Place spareribs on 2 parchment-lined baking sheets. Spread sauce over ribs. Loosely cover ribs with another sheet of parchment paper. Bake in a preheated 350° oven for 1½ hours. Baste occasionally while baking.

SPICY PECANS
Servings: 6

Walnuts can be substituted for pecans and are equally delicious. This can be served as an appetizer or over vanilla ice cream as a dessert.

4 cups pecans, large pieces or halves
2 tbs. egg whites
½ cup sugar
2 tbs. cinnamon

In a large bowl, combine nuts with egg whites. In a separate bowl, mix together sugar and cinnamon. Sprinkle mixture over nuts and stir until nuts are well coated. Spread nuts on a parchment-lined cookie sheet and bake in a preheated 300° oven for 30 minutes. Cool.

STUFFED EGGPLANT
Servings: 16

This dish can be served as an appetizer or as a side dish with the main course.

2 large eggplants
4 eggs
3 cups Italian seasoned breadcrumbs
4 tbs. grated Parmesan cheese
2-3 tbs. olive oil
12 oz. ricotta cheese, or 1½ cups
3 cups tomato sauce
½ cup shredded mozzarella cheese
½ tsp. chopped fresh parsley

Peel eggplants and cut each lengthwise into eight ¼-inch-thick slices. Soak eggplant slices in cold water for 2 minutes; drain. Repeat this process 4 times. Place eggplant slices in a colander and drain for 1 hour. Beat 3 eggs in a shallow bowl. In another shallow bowl, combine breadcrumbs and 1 tbs. Parmesan cheese. Dip eggplant slices in egg and coat with breadcrumbs. Shake off excess.

Heat 1 tbs. olive oil in a large skillet. Fry slices for 2 minutes on each side, adding oil as needed. Remove from pan and place eggplant slices on a paper-towel lined platter. Place paper towels between layers. Continue until all slices are cooked.

Line a deep sided rectangular casserole with parchment paper. In a medium bowl, beat remaining egg and add ricotta cheese. Spread a spoonful of ricotta mixture over each slice of eggplant, leaving a 1/4-inch border on all sides. Roll up eggplant slices and place in casserole. Pour tomato sauce over eggplant and cover with mozzarella cheese. Sprinkle with 3 tbs. Parmesan cheese and parsley. Place a sheet of parchment paper over stuffed eggplant. Bake in a preheated 375° oven for 20 minutes. Remove top sheet of parchment paper and bake for 5 additional minutes.

CHEESE HORNS
Yields: 30

These are a delightful alternative to fried mozzarella sticks. Serve with a spicy marinara sauce for dipping.

¼ cup butter, softened
½ cup shredded Monterey Jack cheese
½ cup shredded cheddar cheese
1 cup flour
1 tbs. chopped fresh basil
2 tbs. water

In a medium bowl, cream together butter and cheese. Blend flour into mixture and add basil. Starting with 1 tablespoon, add water as needed to form dough. Roll dough into thin sheets and cut into 3-inch circles. To form circles into horn shapes, fold two sides of dough circle over each other at an angle. Pinch to hold shape. Place horns on a parchment-lined baking sheet, seam side up. Bake in a preheated 400° oven for 20 minutes.

SHRIMP WITH PEA PODS
Yields: 24

These delicious morsels have the added virtue of being fat-free.

1 cup lemon juice
½ cup sherry
1 tsp. dried dill weed
½ tsp. dried parsley
¼ tsp. freshly ground pepper
2 dozen large shrimp, shelled, deveined
2 dozen snow pea pods

In a small bowl, combine lemon juice, sherry, dill weed, parsley and pepper. Pour marinade over shrimp. Refrigerate for 2 hours. Wrap a pea pod around each shrimp and secure with a wooden pick. Place shrimp with pea pods in a parchment-lined casserole. Drizzle with remaining marinade. Cover casserole with a sheet of parchment paper. Bake in a preheated 375° oven for 20 minutes. Remove parchment cover and serve in casserole or transfer to a warm serving tray.

NACHOS
Yields: 48

Everyone loves nachos, but they're messy and difficult to serve to a large crowd. The parchment paper makes nachos easy to prepare and serve individually.

8 whole wheat or regular tortillas
2 cups shredded cheddar cheese
2 cups shredded Monterey Jack cheese
1 large green bell pepper, finely chopped
1 chili pepper, finely chopped

1 tbs. finely chopped jalapeño pepper
1 medium onion, finely chopped
1/4 cup black ripe olives, finely chopped
1 tsp. chili powder
1 cup sour cream

Cut each tortilla into 6 wedges. Place wedges on a parchment-lined baking sheet and bake in a preheated 350° oven for 10 minutes on each side. Place a layer of cheddar cheese and Monterey Jack on each chip. Cover cheese with peppers, onion, olives and a sprinkle of chili powder. Return to oven and bake until cheese is melted. Serve immediately with sour cream.

SKEWERED SCALLOPS WITH PROSCIUTTO

Servings: 4

This recipe can be served as a tantalizing appetizer or a main course.

4 thin slices prosciutto
1 lb. scallops
1 medium zucchini
1 large onion
1 lb. mushrooms, thinly sliced

½ cup diced scallions
4 tbs. olive oil
2 tbs. minced fresh tarragon
2 garlic cloves, minced

Cut prosciutto into 1-inch-wide strips. Wrap prosciutto strips around scallops. Slice zucchini into ¼-inch rounds. Cut onion into quarters and separate layers. Alternately thread onion, zucchini and scallops onto 4 bamboo skewers. Lay out four 15-x-15-inch sheets of parchment paper and fold in half. Unfold parchment and place a bed of mushrooms and scallions on one side of each sheet next to fold. Place skewer on top of vegetables. Drizzle with olive oil; sprinkle with tarragon and minced garlic. Fold and tightly seal each packet. Place packets on a baking sheet in a preheated 375° oven for 15 minutes. Carefully transfer packets to serving plates, allowing guests to open packets at the table.

PARCHMENT CHICKEN
Yields: 20-22

This is a classic Chinese method for preparing a tasty appetizer or first course. The parchment paper keeps the food hot. These can be prepared in advance and frozen, and then reheated in the packets at 325° for 10 minutes.

2 boneless, skinless chicken breast halves
1 tbs. soy sauce
1 tsp. sherry
2 tbs. minced onion

½ tsp. sesame oil
½ tbs. minced cilantro
½ tsp. orange zest

Rinse chicken and pat dry. Slice chicken into thin ¼-x-½-inch pieces. Combine all ingredients in a shallow bowl and mix thoroughly. Marinate in the refrigerator for 2 to 3 hours. Lay out 22 four-inch-square pieces of parchment paper. Lay each piece of paper at an angle so the corners are at the top, bottom and sides. Place 1 tsp. chicken mixture in center of each paper. Fold up ½-inch of bottom corner. Fold entire bottom corner over mixture. Fold sides into center so they overlap. Fold packet in half, leaving top corner flap free. Tuck in flap to secure packet. (See page 6.) Place packets on a parchment-lined baking sheet in a preheated 400° oven for 17 minutes. Pile packets on a serving platter next to wooden picks. Allow guests to unfold.

SPICY CHICKEN WINGS

Servings: 4

This is a delicious snack or appetizer. The marinade is also wonderful for other cuts of chicken, pork chops, ribs, seafood, turkey and vegetables.

2 lb. chicken wings, about 12
¼ cup soy sauce
½ cup brown sugar
1 clove garlic, minced
1 tsp. ground ginger
1 medium onion, diced
1 tbs. honey

Remove excess skin from wings. Rinse and pat dry. Combine all ingredients in a bowl and mix thoroughly. Marinate chicken for 2 hours or overnight. Line sides and bottom of a shallow baking pan with a sheet of parchment paper. Place chicken wings in pan with ¾ of marinade. Bake in a preheated 450° oven for 45 minutes. Baste occasionally with remaining marinade. Serve hot or cold.

VEGETABLES

TOMATO ZUCCHINI BAKE FOR PASTA

Servings: 2

This dish will absolutely be one of your favorites. It is simple to prepare, spicy and satisfying. Vine ripened or canned plum tomatoes work best. You may substitute fresh beefsteak or cherry tomatoes. Serve this as a side dish or a healthy main course with fresh rolls, green salad and white wine.

1 cup diced plum tomatoes
3 medium zucchini, quartered
2 garlic cloves, crushed
2 tbs. chopped fresh basil, or 1 tbs.
  dried

2 tbs. olive oil
1/8 tsp. freshly ground black pepper
1/8 tsp. dried red pepper flakes
1/8 tsp. minced onions
6 oz. dried angel hair pasta, cooked

In a large bowl, combine all ingredients and blend together. Lay out an 18-x-15-inch sheet of parchment paper and fold in half. Unfold paper and place all ingredients on one side of sheet next to fold. Fold and seal tightly. Place packet on a baking sheet and bake in a preheated 350° oven for 25 minutes. Serve hot over angel hair pasta.

BAKED STUFFED ZUCCHINI
Servings: 6

Here's a change of pace for that ever-abundant zucchini.

6 medium zucchini
1 tbs. butter
1 cup water
½ cup bulghur wheat
1 tbs. olive oil
1 garlic clove, minced
½ tsp. dried basil

1 medium onion, finely chopped
¼ tsp. freshly ground pepper
1 large green or red bell pepper, chopped
1 large tomato, chopped
2 tbs. grated Parmesan cheese

Slice each zucchini in half lengthwise. Scoop pulp out, leaving about ½-inch on edges. Finely chop pulp and set aside. In a small saucepan, melt butter in water. Add bulghur and simmer for 15 minutes. Heat olive oil in a skillet. Sauté garlic, basil, onion and ground pepper for 3 minutes. Add bell pepper, tomato and chopped zucchini pulp. Sauté for 3 minutes. Add bulghur; stir constantly for 2 to 3 minutes. Spoon stuffing into empty zucchini shells. Sprinkle with Parmesan cheese. Individually wrap stuffed zucchini in sheets of parchment paper. Place on a baking sheet and bake in a preheated 350°oven for 30 minutes.

GREEN BEANS AMANDINE

Servings: 4

This is a delicious, yet effortless, twist to a classic dish.

1 lb. fresh green beans
¼ cup almond slices
1 tbs. water
2 tbs. butter

Cut ends off beans. Lay out an 18-x-15-inch sheet of parchment paper and fold in half. Unfold parchment and place beans on one side of fold. Sprinkle with almond slices. Drizzle water over beans and almonds. Dot with butter. Fold parchment and seal tightly. Place package on a baking sheet and bake in a preheated 350° oven for 20 minutes.

RED SKINNED POTATOES
Servings: 4

This is soon to be your favorite method for preparing potatoes. It's convenient, quick, easy and absolutely delicious.

12 medium red skinned potatoes
1 medium onion, sliced
2 garlic cloves, minced
freshly ground pepper

Cut potatoes into 1/4-inch slices. In a large bowl, mix potatoes, onion and garlic. Season with pepper. Lay out an 18-x-15-inch sheet of parchment paper and fold in half. Unfold parchment and place ingredients on one side of paper. Fold and seal tightly. Place package on a baking sheet and bake in a preheated 375° oven for 1 hour.

SCALLOPED POTATOES

Servings: 4

The parchment-lined casserole makes an interesting presentation and makes the dish a cinch to clean.

4 cups peeled, thinly sliced raw potatoes
1 tbs. finely chopped onion
salt and pepper to taste
3 tbs. butter
1¼ cups milk

Line an ovenproof casserole with parchment paper leaving extra paper over sides to prevent food from running over. Lay 3 layers of potatoes in casserole. Sprinkle each layer with onion, salt and pepper and dot with butter. Heat milk and pour over potatoes. Bake uncovered in a preheated 350° oven for 1¼ hours.

VARIATION
For a zesty flavor, sprinkle chopped sun-dried tomatoes between layers of potatoes.

SOUR CREAM AND CHEESE POTATO BAKE
Servings: 6

This cheesy potato dish is rich and delicious. It's perfectly baked in parchment paper.

6 medium red or white potatoes
1 cup sour cream
2 cups cottage cheese
¼ cup chopped fresh chives

¼ tsp. dried parsley
1 tbs. finely chopped onion
½ tsp. freshly ground pepper
½ cup shredded cheddar cheese

Cut potatoes into cubes. Place in a saucepan of cold water and bring to a boil. Reduce heat and simmer for 12 minutes. Line bottom and sides of an ovenproof casserole with parchment paper. In a large bowl, combine potatoes, sour cream, cottage cheese, chives, parsley, onion and pepper. Pour into parchment-lined casserole and cover with parchment paper. Bake in a preheated 375° oven for 30 minutes. Remove parchment cover and sprinkle with cheddar cheese. Return uncovered casserole to oven and bake for 10 minutes.

MUSHROOM-SHAPED NEW POTATOES

Servings: 6

This is a new twist to a classic vegetable. Arrange these around your next pork roast or whole chicken for an elegant and interesting presentation.

18 small new potatoes
2 tbs. olive oil
1 tbs. dried parsley

1 tsp. ground rosemary
freshly ground pepper

Wash potatoes with a vegetable brush. To carve potatoes into mushroom shapes, insert an apple corer into the top center of each potato, 1/2-inch deep, as if you were coring an apple. Carefully remove corer without removing any potato. With a sharp paring knife, make a slit around potato, perpendicular to end of core cut, about 1/2-inch from top of potato. This will release outer top sections of potato leaving only center core and will transform potato into shape of a large mushroom. Place potatoes in a parchment-lined casserole. Drizzle with olive oil and season with parsley, rosemary and pepper. Bake in a preheated 450° oven for 45 minutes.

BAKED ACORN SQUASH
Servings: 2

Baking in parchment paper allows the squash to be cooked in its own natural juices and reduces cooking time. Vitamins are retained and flavor is enhanced.

1 acorn squash
2 tbs. brown sugar
2 tbs. butter

Cut squash in half and remove seeds. Pierce insides of squash with a fork in several places. Place cut sides up and fill each with 1 tbs. brown sugar and 1 tbs. butter. Lay out a 20-x-15-inch sheet of parchment paper and fold in half. Unfold paper and place squash, cut sides up, on one side of parchment next to fold. Fold and seal tightly. Place in a baking dish and bake in a preheated 375° oven for 50 minutes. Serve squash immediately.

VARIATION

Instead of using brown sugar, sprinkle with grated Parmesan cheese for a more savory flavor.

STEAMED BEETS

Servings: 4

Beets cooked in parchment paper retain color and flavor.

1½ lb. beets (2½-inch diameter), root and stem left on
1 tsp. water
2 tsp. butter
2 tsp. fresh orange juice
freshly ground pepper
zest from 1 orange

Carefully wash beets leaving on root and 1 inch of stem. Lay out two 15-x-15-inch sheets of parchment paper and drizzle each sheet with ½ tsp. water. Place half the beets on the center of each sheet. Join corners of sheet together to form a bag. With a piece of string or metal wire, tie each bag securely. Place bags in a pot of boiling water, cover, reduce heat and simmer for 1 hour. Melt butter in a small saucepan. Add orange juice and simmer for 1 minute on low heat. Remove beets from parchment bags. Peel and discard skins. Slice beets and arrange on a platter. Pour sauce over beets and sprinkle with pepper and orange zest.

PARCHMENT BAKED CARROTS
Servings: 4

Available year-round, carrots can be a part of almost any meal. If you haven't tried dill before with cooked carrots, please do. This is an excellent side dish.

6 medium carrots
1 tsp. dried dill weed
2 tbs. butter
4 tbs. water
brown sugar to taste

Peel and cut carrots into 1/4-inch diagonal slices. Lay out an 18-x-15-inch sheet of parchment paper or parchment heart and fold. Unfold parchment and place carrots on one side of sheet next to fold. Season with dill weed, dot with butter and drizzle with water. Sprinkle with brown sugar. Fold and seal tightly. Place package on a baking sheet and bake in a preheated 350° oven for 20 minutes.

TOMATOES IN WHITE WINE

Servings: 4

Serve this as a vegetable side dish with poultry or fish.

4 firm medium tomatoes
4 tsp. white wine
1 tsp. chopped cilantro
1 tbs. grated Parmesan cheese
freshly ground pepper

Lay out four 15-x-15-inch sheets of parchment paper. Place 1 tomato in the center of each sheet. Pour 1 tsp. wine over each tomato and sprinkle with cilantro. Join corners of each sheet together to form a bag. With a piece of string or metal wire, tie each bag securely. Place bags on a baking sheet and bake in a preheated 350° oven for 30 minutes. Transfer to serving plates and serve in parchment paper. Sprinkle with Parmesan cheese and pepper.

BRUSSELS SPROUTS
Servings: 4

This is a delicious treatment for Brussels sprouts. Precious vitamins and minerals are not thrown out with the cooking water!

1 lb. Brussels sprouts
1 tsp. water
2 tbs. butter
½ cup coarsely chopped walnuts
¼ tsp. ground rosemary

Wash sprouts; trim off wilted leaves and cut in half. Lay out two 15-x-15-inch sheets of parchment paper and drizzle with water. Place half of sprouts in center of each sheet. Join corners of each sheet together to form a bag. With a piece of string or metal wire, tie each bag securely. Place bags in a pot of boiling water and cover. Reduce heat and simmer for 12 minutes. While sprouts cook, melt butter in a sauté pan. Add walnuts and rosemary and sauté for 4 minutes. Pour over cooked sprouts.

GREEN BEANS WITH ROSEMARY AND THYME

Servings: 2

Flavorful, crunchy and healthy, the beans never come in contact with the boiling water.

¾ lb. fresh green beans
1 tsp. water
½ tsp. dried rosemary
½ tsp. dried thyme
2 tsp. butter

Wash beans and cut into 2-inch pieces. Lay out two 15-x-15-inch sheets of parchment paper and drizzle with water. Place half of beans in the center of each sheet of parchment paper. Sprinkle with rosemary and thyme. Dot with butter. Join corners of each sheet together to form a bag. With a piece of string or metal wire, tie each bag securely. Place bags in a pot of boiling water and cover. Reduce heat and simmer for 50 minutes.

PARCHMENT BROCCOLI

Servings: 4

Parchment makes perfect, bright green, crisp and healthy broccoli every time. The broccoli cooks in its own juice and never comes in contact with the water, retaining all the nutrients and flavor. The bags are insoluble and allow broccoli to remain hot until opened by your guests.

1 lb. fresh broccoli
2 tbs. water
1 garlic clove, minced

¼ tsp. freshly ground pepper
2 tbs. grated Parmesan cheese

Chop broccoli florets into 1-inch pieces and cut stems into small julienne matchstick strips. This should equal 4 or 5 cups. Lay out four 15-x-15-inch sheets of parchment paper and drizzle each sheet with ½ tbs. water. Place equal amounts of broccoli in the center of each sheet. Top with garlic, season with pepper and sprinkle with Parmesan cheese. Join corners of each sheet together to form a bag. With a piece of string or metal wire, tie each bag securely. Place bags in a pot of boiling water, cover, reduce heat and simmer for 12 minutes. Transfer bags to serving plates.

PARCHMENT ASPARAGUS

Servings: 4

To retain flavor, asparagus should always be cooked and eaten as soon as possible.

2 bunches asparagus
1 tsp. water

Carefully wash asparagus. Use a brush to remove dirt, if necessary. Peel off skin and cut off tough ends. Cut asparagus into 1½-inch pieces. This should produce about 3 cups. Lay out two 15-x-15-inch sheets of parchment paper and drizzle with water. Place half of asparagus on center of each sheet. Join corners of each sheet together to form a bag. With a piece of string or metal wire, tie each bag securely. Place bags in a pot of boiling water and cover. Reduce heat and simmer for 25 minutes. Serve with *Hollandaise Sauce*, page 137, or butter and freshly ground pepper.

BROCCOLI SOUFFLÉ
Servings: 6

A solid copper bowl and a quality French balloon whisk are ideal for beating egg whites.

¼ cup butter, melted
1 cup milk
¼ cup flour
⅛ tsp. salt
¼ tsp. freshly ground pepper
⅛ tsp. ground cinnamon

1 tbs. finely chopped onion
3 eggs, separated
1 cup chopped cooked broccoli
1 tsp. cream of tartar
1 tsp. vegetable oil
⅛ tsp. confectioners' sugar

In a medium bowl, combine butter, milk, flour, salt, pepper, cinnamon and onion. Add egg yolks, 1 at a time, while continuously mixing. Add broccoli and mix. In a large bowl, beat egg whites and cream of tartar until stiff peaks form. Fold in broccoli mixture. Fit a 15-x-15-inch sheet of parchment paper into a 1½-quart soufflé dish. Brush parchment paper with oil. Fold edges of parchment over sides of dish. Pour mixture into dish. Bake in a preheated 350° oven for 20 minutes. Quickly sprinkle top of soufflé with confectioners' sugar and bake for 30 more minutes. Serve at once.

NOTE: For a traditional presentation, rather than using the 15-x-15-inch sheet of parchment paper, support the sides with a parchment soufflé collar (see page 9).

STUFFED PEPPERS
Servings: 6

Parchment prevents the peppers and stuffing from drying out.

6 extra large green or red bell peppers
1 tbs. olive oil
1 garlic clove, minced
1 medium onion, finely chopped
1/4 cup chopped broccoli
1/4 cup sliced mushrooms
1 can (2.25 oz.) ripe black olives,
  finely chopped
1/8 tsp. dried basil
1/8 tsp. freshly ground pepper
3/4 cup tomato sauce
3 cups cooked rice
1/4 cup shredded Monterey Jack cheese
1/2 cup shredded mozzarella cheese
1/4 tsp. chopped fresh parsley

Cut off tops of peppers. Remove seeds and membranes. Parboil peppers for 2 minutes. Heat oil in a large skillet; add garlic, onion, broccoli, mushrooms, olives, basil and ground pepper. Sauté for 5 minutes. Add tomato sauce and cooked rice. Sauté for 2 minutes and remove from heat. Spoon mixture into cavity of each pepper. Place peppers in a parchment-lined casserole dish. Top each pepper with cheeses and sprinkle with parsley. Cover casserole with a sheet of parchment paper. Bake in a preheated 350° oven for 30 minutes. Remove top sheet of parchment and bake for an additional 10 minutes.

SWEET-AND-SOUR VEGETABLES
Servings: 4

This is an easy and healthy method for preparing spicy vegetables.

1 large red bell pepper
1 large green bell pepper
1 cup sliced mushrooms
¼ cup thinly sliced water chestnuts
4 scallions, chopped
2 celery stalks, chopped
2 carrots, thinly sliced
1 garlic clove, minced
1 tsp. minced fresh ginger root
2 tbs. water
½ cup pineapple juice
2 tbs. lemon juice
1 tbs. red wine vinegar
2 tbs. honey
1 tsp. light soy sauce

Slice peppers into matchstick strips. In a large bowl, combine peppers, mushrooms, chestnuts, scallions, celery, carrots, garlic and ginger root. Lay out two 18-x-15-inch sheets of parchment paper and fold in half. Unfold parchment sheets and place half of vegetables on one side of each sheet next to fold. Drizzle 1 tbs. water over vegetables. Fold and seal tightly. Place packets on a baking sheet and bake in a preheated 375° oven for 20 minutes.

Combine pineapple juice, lemon juice, vinegar, honey and soy sauce in a small saucepan and heat. Transfer cooked vegetables to a large serving bowl and spoon sauce over vegetables.

VEGETABLE MEDLEY
Servings: 4

This is a fast and easy way to cook vegetables that can go with almost any meal.

2 cups thinly sliced carrots
2 cups thinly sliced zucchini
1 cup prepared broccoli (chopped florets, sliced stems)
1 medium tomato, diced
1 medium onion, thinly sliced
¼ cup sliced almonds

¼ tsp. dried basil
⅛ tsp. freshly ground pepper
½ cup water
4 tbs. butter
3 tsp. brown sugar
2 tsp. dried parsley

In a large bowl, mix together carrots, zucchini, broccoli, tomato, onion, almonds, basil and pepper. Lay out two 18-x-15-inch sheets of parchment paper and fold in half. Unfold parchment and place half of vegetables on one side of each sheet next to fold. Drizzle vegetables with water. Fold and seal tightly. Place parchment packets on a baking sheet and bake in a preheated 350° oven for 20 minutes. While vegetables are cooking, melt butter in a small saucepan. Mix in brown sugar. Add parsley and simmer on low heat until vegetables are ready. Pour sauce over cooked vegetables.

MEDITERRANEAN EGGPLANT

Servings: 6

Serve this with angel hair pasta and fresh bread.

1 medium eggplant
1 tbs. olive oil
1/4 cup chopped onion
2 garlic cloves, peeled, halved
3/4 cup peeled, seeded, chopped tomatoes
1 cup stewed tomatoes with juice
1/4 cup unsalted peanuts

1/4 tsp. freshly ground pepper
1/4 tsp. dried oregano
1/4 tsp. dried basil
1 tsp. chopped fresh cilantro
1/4 cup water
1/2 tsp. lime juice
1/4 cup white wine

Peel and slice eggplant lengthwise into 8 wedges. Soak wedges in cold water for 2 minutes; drain. Repeat this process 4 times. Place eggplant in a colander and drain for 1 hour. Lay out two 15-x-18-inch sheets of parchment paper and fold in half. Unfold parchment and brush a light coat of olive oil inside each sheet. Place 4 eggplant wedges on one side of each sheet next to fold. Fold and tightly seal each packet. Place packets on a baking sheet and bake in a preheated 350° oven for 20 minutes. In a food processor or blender, combine remaining ingredients. Puree until well blended and heat in a saucepan. Transfer cooked eggplant to serving plates. Pour sauce over eggplant.

EGGPLANT PARMESAN
Servings: 6

The next time you make this old favorite, use parchment paper.

1 large eggplant
2 eggs
2 tbs. grated Parmesan cheese
1½ cups seasoned breadcrumbs

3 tbs. olive oil
3 cups tomato sauce
½ cup shredded mozzarella cheese
⅛ tsp. chopped parsley

Peel eggplant and cut into ⅛-inch round slices. Soak slices in cold water for 2 minutes; drain. Repeat process 4 times. Place eggplant in a colander and drain for 1 hour. Beat eggs in a shallow bowl. Add 1 tbs. Parmesan cheese to breadcrumbs and mix. Dip eggplant slices in egg and coat with breadcrumbs. Shake off excess. Heat 1 tbs. oil in a large skillet. Fry slices for 2 minutes on each side. Add oil as needed. Remove from pan and pile on a platter lined with paper towels. Place paper towels between layers; continue until all slices are cooked. Line a deep casserole dish with parchment paper. Arrange a layer of eggplant slices on bottom; cover with tomato sauce and sprinkle with mozzarella cheese. Repeat with remaining eggplant. Sprinkle with mozzarella cheese, remaining Parmesan and parsley. Cover with a sheet of parchment paper. Bake in a preheated 375° oven for 15 minutes. Remove top sheet of parchment and bake for 5 more minutes.

POULTRY

CHICKEN MONARI
Servings: 4

Sun-dried tomatoes, black olives, mushrooms and chicken combine for a spectacular dinner. Serve with fresh pasta and a green salad.

4 boneless, skinless chicken breast halves
1/2 cup skim milk
1/2 cup seasoned breadcrumbs
2 tbs. olive oil
1 1/2 cups sliced mushrooms
1/3 cup sliced black olives
2 garlic cloves, minced
1/2 cup chopped sun-dried tomatoes, reconstituted
1/2 tsp. dried oregano
1/4 tsp. freshly ground pepper
1/2 cup tomato sauce
1/4 cup shredded mozzarella cheese

Rinse chicken and pat dry. Pour milk into a shallow dish and dip chicken in milk. Coat each side of chicken with bread crumbs and shake off excess. Heat 1 tbs. oil in a skillet and sauté chicken for 1 minute each side. Remove chicken from skillet and set aside. Heat 1 tbs. oil in skillet and sauté mushrooms for 3 minutes. Add remaining ingredients except chicken and cheese and sauté for 3 additional minutes.

Lay out four 18-x-15-inch sheets of parchment paper or 4 hearts. Unfold papers and spoon 1/8 tomato mixture on one side of each sheet next to fold. Place chicken breast on top and sprinkle with mozzarella cheese. Spoon remaining tomato mixture over chicken. Fold and tightly seal. Place packets on a baking sheet and bake in a preheated 375° oven for 30 minutes. Transfer packets to individual serving plates, allowing guests to open packets at the table.

CHICKEN OREGANOTO

Servings: 4

This perfectly flavored entrée is one of my favorites. Don't be alarmed by the quantity of oregano. It works! Serve with **Parchment Baked Carrots**, *page 44.*

4 boneless, skinless chicken breast
  halves
½ cup skim milk
½ cup seasoned breadcrumbs
2 tbs. olive oil

2 tbs. butter
2 garlic cloves, crushed
2 tbs. dried oregano
¼ cup dry sherry, optional
8 tomato slices, ⅛-inch thick

Rinse chicken and pat dry. Pour milk into a shallow dish and dip chicken in milk. Coat each side of chicken with bread crumbs and shake off excess. Heat oil in a skillet, sauté chicken for 1 minute each side and set aside. Melt butter in a small saucepan. Add garlic, oregano and sherry. Mix and set aside. Lay out two 18-x-15-inch sheets of parchment paper or 2 hearts and fold in half. Unfold papers and place 2 chicken breasts on one side of each sheet next to fold. Do not let chicken overlap. Layer tomato slices on top of chicken. Slowly pour oregano sauce over tomatoes and chicken. Fold and seal tightly. Place packets on a baking sheet and bake in a preheated 375° oven for 30 minutes.

SESAME LEMON CHICKEN
Servings: 4

If you like the flavor of Oriental cooking, you'll love this dish. It is spicy, aromatic and easy to prepare. Serve it over white rice.

4 boneless, skinless chicken breast
  halves
2 tbs. sesame seeds

½ cup light soy sauce
2 garlic cloves, minced
juice of 1 lemon

Rinse chicken and pat dry. Roast sesame seeds in a dry skillet over medium heat, stirring constantly until seeds are golden brown. Combine soy sauce, garlic and 5 tsp. sesame seeds in a bowl and mix. Place chicken in a shallow dish. Pour marinade over chicken, turning each piece to coat. Marinate for 2 hours in the refrigerator. Lay out two 18-x-15-inch sheets of parchment paper or 2 hearts and fold in half. Unfold sheets and place 2 chicken breasts on one side of each sheet next to fold. Do not let chicken overlap. Pour remaining marinade over chicken. Drizzle with lemon juice and sprinkle remaining sesame seeds over each piece of chicken. Fold and seal tightly. Place each packet on a baking sheet and bake in a preheated 400° oven for 25 minutes. Remove from packets to warm plates to serve.

SPINACH STUFFED CHICKEN BREASTS
Servings: 4

The parchment locks in the juices and the flavors are preserved. Serve it with brown rice and steamed vegetables.

4 cups chopped fresh spinach, trimmed, stems removed
1/4 cup white wine
2 garlic cloves, minced
4 boneless, skinless chicken breast halves
1/2 cup skim milk
3/4 cup bread crumbs
2 tbs. butter
salt and pepper to taste

Place spinach in a bowl with white wine and garlic. Mix and set aside. Rinse chicken and pat dry. Flatten each chicken breast between 2 pieces parchment paper with a wooden mallet. Place 1 cup spinach on top of each chicken breast. Roll each chicken breast tightly and secure with wooden picks. Dip stuffed chicken into milk and coat with bread crumbs.

Lay out four 18-x-15-inch sheets of parchment paper or 4 hearts and fold. Unfold each sheet and dot paper with ½ tbs. butter. Place a stuffed chicken breast on each parchment sheet next to fold. Pour remaining wine from bowl over chicken. Season with salt and pepper. Fold and tightly seal each packet. Place packets on a baking sheet and bake in a preheated 375° oven for 30 minutes. Transfer packets to individual serving plates, allowing guests to open packets at the table.

CHICKEN MARSALA
Servings: 4

This recipe lends itself very nicely to cooking in parchment paper. Serve it with fresh pasta.

4 boneless, skinless chicken breast halves
¼ cup skim milk
½ cup seasoned breadcrumbs
3 tbs. olive oil
2 medium green bell peppers, sliced into ¼-x-1½-inch pieces
2 medium onions, thinly sliced
½ lb. mushrooms, thinly sliced
1 garlic clove, minced
½ cup Marsala wine
1 lemon, thinly sliced

Rinse chicken and pat dry. Flatten chicken breasts between 2 pieces of parchment paper with a wooden mallet. In a shallow dish, dip chicken into milk. Coat chicken on both sides with breadcrumbs and shake off excess. Heat oil in a skillet and sauté chicken for 1 minute on each side. Combine peppers, onions, mushrooms, garlic and wine in a large bowl.

Lay out two 18-x-15-inch sheets of parchment paper or 2 hearts and fold in half. Unfold sheets and place ¼ pepper-onion mixture on one side of each sheet next to fold. Place 2 chicken breasts on top of vegetables on each sheet. Do not let chicken overlap. Evenly cover chicken with remaining vegetables and liquid. Arrange 2 or 3 lemon slices on top. Fold and tightly seal. Place packets on a baking sheet and bake in a preheated 375° oven for 30 minutes.

SCARBOROUGH FAIR ROASTED CHICKEN
Servings: 4

The parchment-wrapped chicken bakes in its own natural juices. The results are tender, moist and delicious. The stuffing is a tantalizing blend of herbs. Somewhat inspired by Paul Simon, this dish will be a "true love of yours".

STUFFING

½ cup butter
½ cup finely chopped celery
½ cup finely chopped onion
4 cups breadcrumbs
¼ tsp. dried oregano

⅛ tsp. dried parsley
⅛ tsp. dried sage
⅛ tsp. dried, crushed rosemary
⅛ tsp. dried thyme
⅛ tsp. dried marjoram

In a large skillet, melt butter. Add celery and onion and sauté until tender, about 5 to 7 minutes. Combine breadcrumbs and herbs in a large bowl and mix thoroughly. Add onions, celery and butter. Toss to combine.

4 lb. roasting chicken
1 garlic clove, thinly sliced
1 tbs. olive oil
1/4 tsp. dried thyme
1/8 tsp. ground pepper
1 onion, thinly sliced

Preheat oven to 375°. Remove giblets from chicken. Rinse chicken and pat dry. Stuff chicken and truss. Tuck garlic slices under skin and rub skin with olive oil. Season with thyme and pepper, top with onion slices and wrap chicken with a 30-x-15-inch sheet of parchment paper. Place in a 2-inch-deep baking dish, breast side up. Bake for 2½ to 3 hours or until an instant read thermometer reads 180° when inserted into thigh of bird. Remove from oven and let stand for 15 minutes before carving.

LEMON THYME CHICKEN
Servings: 4

This chicken is great with linguine and broccoli.

4 boneless, skinless chicken breast halves
½ cup skim milk
½ cup breadcrumbs
2 tbs. olive oil
1 medium onion, thinly sliced
1½ cups thinly sliced mushrooms
2 cups water
juice of ½ lemon
2 chicken-flavored bouillon cubes
1 tsp. dried thyme
3-4 tbs. flour

Rinse chicken and pat dry. Pour milk into a shallow dish. Dip chicken into milk, coat with breadcrumbs and shake off excess. Heat oil in a skillet and sauté chicken for 2 minutes on each side. Lay out four 18-x-15-inch sheets of parchment paper or 4 parchment hearts and fold in half. Unfold parchment and place ¼ onion slices on one side of each sheet next to fold. Arrange a chicken breast over onion and scatter mushrooms over chicken. In a small saucepan, combine water, lemon juice, bouillon cubes, thyme and flour. Simmer for at least 5 minutes. Pour 3 tbs. liquid over chicken in each packet. Fold and seal tightly. Place packets on baking sheets and bake in a preheated 375° oven for 30 minutes. While chicken bakes, keep remaining sauce warm. Remove packets from oven and transfer to individual serving plates. Pour sauce over chicken.

ORIENTAL-STYLE CHICKEN AND VEGETABLES
Servings: 2

Chinese cooking without the messy wok makes this spicy meal quick and easy.

2 boneless, skinless chicken breast
  halves
1 medium onion, thinly sliced
2 cups fresh pea pods, or 6 oz. frozen,
  thawed
3 large carrots, peeled, cut into thin
  matchstick strips

1 medium zucchini, cut into thin
  matchstick strips
¼ cup soy sauce
2 garlic cloves, minced
½ tsp. grated ginger root

Rinse chicken, pat dry and cut into 1-inch cubes. Combine all ingredients in a large bowl. Marinate in the refrigerator for 2 hours. Drain and reserve marinade. Lay out two 18-x-15-inch sheets of parchment paper or 2 hearts and fold. Place half of chicken and vegetables on each unfolded paper next to fold. Slowly pour remaining marinade over chicken and vegetables. Fold and tightly seal packets. Place packets on a baking sheet and bake in a preheated 375° oven for 30 minutes. Serve over white rice.

ORANGE GINGER CHICKEN

Servings: 4

The combined flavors of orange and ginger are especially good with poultry. This is also a delicious treatment for turkey tenderloins.

4 boneless, skinless chicken breast halves
1 cup frozen orange juice concentrate, thawed
2 tsp. grated fresh ginger root
4 tsp. light soy sauce
1/4 cup butter, melted
1/4 tsp. freshly ground pepper
1/4 tsp. dried parsley

Rinse chicken and pat dry. In a small bowl, combine juice concentrate, ginger, soy sauce, butter, pepper and parsley. Arrange chicken in a parchment-lined casserole dish. Spread sauce over chicken. Cover chicken with a layer of parchment paper. Bake in a preheated 375° oven for 30 minutes.

PESTO CHICKEN
Servings: 4

Since pesto freezes so well, I recommend making a large batch and freezing the extra. Freeze the pesto without cheese and add the cheese after the pesto defrosts. Serve this with pasta, salad and hot crusty bread.

2 cups fresh basil leaves
3 garlic cloves
1 cup plus 1 tbs. olive oil
½ cup pine nuts, or chopped walnuts
¼ tsp. freshly ground pepper
½ cup grated Parmesan cheese
2 boneless, skinless chicken breast halves
1 can (2.25 oz.) sliced black ripe olives, optional

To make pesto, combine basil, garlic, 1 cup olive oil, nuts and pepper in a food processor or blender. Process for 15 to 20 seconds or until paste forms. Pour into a bowl and mix in cheese.

Wash chicken and pat dry. Heat 1 tbs. olive oil in a skillet and sauté chicken on both sides for 2 minutes. Lay out an 18-x-15-inch sheet of parchment paper or 1 parchment heart and fold in half. Unfold parchment and place chicken breasts on one side of sheet next to fold. Do not let chicken overlap. Spread ¼ cup pesto over each chicken breast and top with a layer of olives. Fold and tightly seal parchment paper. Place packet on a baking sheet and bake in a preheated 375° oven for 30 minutes. Pour remaining pesto into individual ramekins for dipping.

LEMON GARLIC PEPPER CHICKEN
Servings: 4

This chicken adds a refreshing lemon taste to an intense garlic and pepper flavor. Serve it with angel hair pasta and sautéed vegetables.

2 boneless, skinless chicken breast
  halves
1 tbs. olive oil
⅛ cup white wine
2 tbs. lemon juice

½ tsp. freshly ground pepper
⅛ tsp. dried coriander
⅛ tsp. dried thyme
3 garlic cloves, crushed
¼ tsp. chopped fresh parsley

Rinse chicken and pat dry. Heat oil in a skillet and sauté chicken for 2 minutes on each side. In a small bowl, combine wine, lemon juice, pepper, coriander, thyme and garlic. Mix to form thick sauce. Lay out an 18-x-15-inch sheet of parchment paper or 1 parchment heart and fold in half. Unfold parchment and place chicken breasts on one side of sheet next to fold. Do not let chicken overlap. Spread equal amounts of sauce over each breast. Sprinkle with parsley. Fold and tightly seal paper. Place packet on a baking sheet and bake in a preheated 375° oven for 30 minutes.

CHICKEN WITH SUN-DRIED TOMATOES

Servings: 4

This recipe comes together perfectly. Serve it with fresh pasta.

4 boneless, skinless chicken breast
  halves
1 tbs. olive oil
juice of 1 lemon
2 garlic cloves, minced

¼ cup fresh minced parsley
8-12 sun-dried tomatoes
2 tbs. butter
freshly ground pepper

Rinse chicken and pat dry. Heat oil in a skillet and sauté chicken for 2 minutes on each side. Lay out two 18-x-15-inch sheets of parchment paper or 2 parchment hearts and fold in half. Unfold parchment and place 2 chicken breasts on one side of each sheet next to fold. Do not let chicken overlap. Cover chicken with lemon juice, garlic and parsley. Blanch sun-dried tomatoes by placing them in a pot of boiling water for 2 minutes. Arrange layer of tomatoes on top of chicken. Dot with butter and season with pepper. Fold and seal tightly. Place packets on a baking sheet and bake in a preheated 375° oven for 30 minutes.

CHICKEN WITH CAPERS
Servings: 4

This blend of interesting ingredients creates a flavorful dish with eye appeal.

4 boneless, skinless chicken breast halves
2 tbs. olive oil
4 tbs. white wine
2 tbs. capers
1/2 tsp. dried basil
salt and freshly ground pepper
8 lemon slices, thinly sliced

Rinse chicken, pat dry and slice into 1-inch strips. Heat olive oil in a skillet and sauté chicken for 2 to 3 minutes. Lay out four 18-x-15-inch sheets of parchment paper or 4 hearts and fold in half. Unfold parchment sheets and spread 1/4 chicken on one side of each sheet next to fold. Pour wine over chicken. Sprinkle with capers and basil. Season with salt and pepper and top with lemon slices. Fold and seal tightly. Place packets on a baking sheet and bake in a preheated 375° oven for 25 minutes. Transfer packets to individual serving plates, allowing guests to open packets at the table.

CHICKEN VEGETABLE MEDLEY

Servings: 4

The scrumptious results will delight you. Serve this over steamed white rice. For variety, leave the breasts whole and brown them before baking en papillote.

4 boneless, skinless chicken breast halves
2 medium carrots, cut into thin matchstick strips
2 medium green, yellow or red bell peppers, cut into thin matchstick strips
½ cup sliced scallions

2 medium yellow crookneck squash, cut into thin matchstick strips
2 cups snap peas, or pea pods
½ lb. mushrooms, thinly sliced
½ tsp. dried basil
2 tbs. grated lemon peel
salt and pepper to taste
4 tbs. butter

Rinse chicken, pat dry and cut into 1-inch pieces. Combine all ingredients except butter in a large bowl. Lay out two 18-x-15-inch sheets of parchment paper or 2 hearts and fold. Unfold parchment sheets and place half of vegetables on one side of each sheet next to fold. Place butter over contents. Fold and seal tightly. Place packets on a baking sheet and bake in a preheated 375° oven for 25 minutes. Top of paper will be lightly brown. Cut open paper and remove contents with a large spoon.

SALSA CHICKEN
Servings: 4

Prepare the salsa the night before or at least 2 hours in advance and refrigerate. Serve as an appetizer with tortilla chips and reserve 1 cup for topping the chicken. The flavor of the salsa is intensified when baked in parchment, creating a spicy and exciting chicken dish. This is one of my favorites. Serve it with rice and salad.

SALSA

1 can (1 lb. 12 oz.) crushed tomatoes in puree
3 garlic cloves, minced
1 medium onion, finely chopped
2 tbs. chopped jalapeño pepper
1 tbs. chili powder

In a large bowl, mix tomatoes, garlic, onion, pepper and chili powder. Refrigerate for at least 2 hours.

4 boneless, skinless chicken breast halves
2 tbs. olive oil
fresh cilantro sprigs for garnish

Rinse chicken and pat dry. Heat olive oil in a skillet and sauté chicken on each side for 2 minutes. Lay out two 18-x-15-inch sheets of parchment paper or 2 parchment hearts and fold. Unfold each sheet and place 2 chicken breasts on one side of each sheet next to fold. Leave 1 inch between chicken breasts. Spread ¼ cup salsa over each breast. Fold and tightly seal packets. Place on a baking sheet and bake in a preheated 375° oven for 30 minutes. Garnish with fresh cilantro. Pour extra salsa into individual ramekins for dipping.

CAJUN CHICKEN
Servings: 4

It's fun to serve each packet on individual plates. As your guests cut into the paper, the steam released has an exciting Cajun aroma. Serve this with corn bread.

4 boneless, skinless chicken breast halves
1 tbs. olive oil
4 medium red or green bell peppers, thinly sliced
Cajun Seasoning, follows

Rinse chicken and pat dry. Heat oil in a skillet and sauté chicken on both sides for 2 minutes and set aside. Lay out four 18-x-15-inch sheets of parchment paper or 4 hearts and fold in half. Unfold parchment and spread 1/4 peppers on one side of each sheet next to fold. Place chicken on top of peppers. Sprinkle each chicken breast with *Cajun Seasoning*. Fold and tightly seal parchment packets. Place packets on a baking sheet and bake in a preheated 400° oven for 30 minutes.

CAJUN SEASONING

1 tsp. salt
1 tsp. white pepper
1 tsp. black pepper
2 tsp. dried oregano
2 tsp. dried thyme

1 tsp. cayenne pepper
1 tsp. chili powder
1 tsp. garlic powder
1 tsp. onion powder
1 tsp. paprika

Combine all ingredients in a small bowl and use sparingly on chicken.

ROAST TURKEY WITH MUSHROOM STUFFING
Servings: 4

Roasting a turkey in parchment paper prevents the bird from drying out and produces a tender, moist and perfectly browned turkey every time.

MUSHROOM STUFFING

½ lb. butter
6 tbs. diced onion
4 tbs. diced celery
4 cups diced mushrooms
8 cups breadcrumbs
¼ tsp. freshly ground pepper

Melt butter in a large skillet and sauté onion, celery and mushrooms until tender. Combine with breadcrumbs and pepper. Mix gently. Do not stuff turkey until you are ready to cook it.

1 turkey, 8 lb.

Preheat oven to 325°. Remove giblets from turkey. Rinse bird and pat dry. Spoon stuffing loosely into cavities and truss. Completely line bottom and sides of a roasting pan with parchment paper. Place turkey, breast side down, in pan. Fold in half an 18-x-15-inch sheet of parchment paper. Unfold paper and cover turkey with a tent-shaped sheet of parchment, so it fits loosely with an open gap at sides and ends of pan. Place turkey in oven. After 1 hour, turn bird on its back. Cover with parchment tent and roast 1 hour more. With an instant-read meat thermometer, check for doneness by inserting thermometer into thigh. Thermometer should read 185°. Wait 15 minutes before carving.

CHICKEN WITH STEWED TOMATOES
Servings: 4

This is a great dish served with fresh pasta.

1 lb. mushrooms, thinly sliced
¼ cup sherry
2 tbs. olive oil
4 boneless, skinless chicken breast
  halves

2 medium zucchini, cut into thin matchstick strips about 2 inches long
½ cup shredded mozzarella cheese
1 can (14.5 oz.) stewed tomatoes, diced
4 garlic cloves, minced

Marinate sliced mushrooms in sherry for 1 hour. Heat oil in a skillet and sauté chicken on each side for 1 minute. Lay out two 18-x-15-inch sheets of parchment paper or 2 hearts and fold. Unfold each sheet of parchment and place half of zucchini on one side of each sheet next to fold. Place 2 chicken breasts on each bed of zucchini. Do not overlap chicken. Drain mushrooms in a colander and discard sherry. Cover each chicken breast with cheese, tomatoes, mushrooms and garlic. Fold and tightly seal each packet. Place packets on a baking sheet and bake in a preheated 375° oven for 30 minutes.

MEATS

SAUSAGE AND PEPPERS
Servings: 4

Find a good Italian meat market and try this recipe with provolone sausage or a sweet sausage with fennel.

1 lb. Italian sausage
2 medium green bell peppers, sliced
1 medium onion, sliced
¼ tsp. dried basil
ground pepper to taste
1 tsp. olive oil

Cut sausage into 1-inch pieces. Brown in a skillet for 3 to 4 minutes. Lay out an 18-x-15-inch sheet of parchment paper and fold in half. Unfold parchment and place half of peppers and onion on one side of each sheet. Place sausage on top of peppers and onion. Do not overlap sausage. Cover sausage with remaining peppers and onion. Season with basil and pepper and drizzle with olive oil. Fold and seal tightly. Place packet on a baking sheet and bake in a preheated 375° oven for 45 minutes.

PORK CHOPS WITH PINEAPPLE

Servings: 4

Prepare the marinade in the morning, marinate the chops while you're away for the day, and pop them in the oven in their paper-lined casserole when you get home. Easy dinner, easy cleanup! Add a green vegetable and some new potatoes.

1/4 cup light soy sauce
1 can (8 oz.) pineapple chunks with juice
2 tbs. brown sugar
1 tbs. sesame oil
2 garlic cloves, minced

1/4 tsp. freshly ground pepper
4 thick pork chops
1 large onion, chopped
2 medium carrots, thinly sliced
1/4 tsp. dried marjoram

Combine soy sauce, pineapple, sugar, oil, garlic and pepper in a small bowl. Place pork chops in a shallow dish. Pour sauce over pork chops and marinate in the refrigerator for at least 4 hours. Line an ovenproof casserole with parchment paper. Arrange onion and carrots in casserole. Place chops and sauce over onions and carrots. Sprinkle with marjoram. Tightly cover casserole with a sheet of parchment paper. Bake in a preheated 350° oven for 45 minutes.

ROAST PORK WITH SAUSAGE STUFFING
Servings: 8

The parchment paper prevents the roast from drying out so it's flavorful, tender and delicious. Try cutting the potatoes into mushroom shapes (see page 41) for an elegant offering to guests.

4 lb. boned, tied double loin roast
1 garlic clove, thinly sliced
1 tbs. olive oil
¼ tsp. dried rosemary

⅛ tsp. freshly ground pepper
1 medium onion, thinly sliced
10 medium new potatoes
Sausage Stuffing, follows

Untie roast and remove exterior fat. Place roast in a parchment-lined roasting pan. Pierce the roast with the tip of a sharp knife. Insert garlic slices and spread a layer of *Sausage Stuffing* between roast pieces. Rub roast with olive oil and season with rosemary and pepper. Surround with onion slices and potatoes. Cover roast with a 15-x-15-inch sheet of parchment paper. Bake in a preheated 350° oven for 2½ hours. Check temperature of pork with an instant-read meat thermometer. It should read 160°. Remove roast from oven and remove parchment paper cover. Wait at least 10 minutes before carving to allow juices to settle so meat will be easier to slice.

SAUSAGE STUFFING

1/4 lb. sweet Italian sausage
1 stalk celery, finely chopped
1 small onion, finely chopped
1 medium tomato, finely chopped
1/4 tsp. dried basil
1/4 tsp. dried thyme
1/4 tsp. freshly ground pepper
4 cups breadcrumbs

Chop sausage into small pieces and sauté for 4 minutes. Add celery and onion and sauté for 4 more minutes. Add tomato, basil, thyme and pepper. Sauté for 4 additional minutes. Add breadcrumbs and mix. Arrange stuffing between layers of roast.

PORK CHOPS WITH DIJON MUSTARD
Servings: 4

This is a mustard-lover's delight!

3 tbs. Dijon mustard
6 tbs. lemon juice
¼ cup light soy sauce
1 tbs. butter
2 medium onions, chopped
4 thick pork chops
½ tsp. freshly ground pepper

In a small bowl, combine mustard, lemon juice and soy sauce. Melt butter in a skillet and brown pork chops quickly on both sides. Line an ovenproof casserole with parchment paper. Scatter onions in casserole. Arrange chops over onions and top with sauce. Season with pepper. Cover casserole with a sheet of parchment paper and bake in a preheated 350° oven for 45 minutes.

PORK CHOPS WITH APPLES AND POTATOES

Servings: 4

This is another tasty treatment for pork chops. Just add a salad and dinner is ready.

4 cups potatoes, peeled, sliced
1 tbs. butter
4 thick pork chops
2 large apples, cored, thinly sliced
1 medium onion, chopped

2 stalks celery, thinly sliced
½ tsp. dried marjoram
¼ tsp. dried thyme
¼ tsp. dried sage
½ tsp. freshly ground pepper

Cook potatoes in a saucepan of boiling water for about 12 minutes or until tender. Melt butter in a skillet and brown pork chops quickly on both sides. In a large bowl, combine potatoes with half the apples. Add onion, celery, herbs and pepper and combine. Line the bottom of an ovenproof 2-quart casserole with parchment paper. Spoon mixture into casserole. Place pork chops on top of potatoes and apples. Arrange remaining apple slices on top of chops. Tightly cover with a sheet of parchment paper and bake in a preheated 350° oven for 45 minutes.

STUFFED VEAL ROLLS
Servings: 2

These tender little veal bundles are melt-in-your-mouth delicious.

2 tbs. butter
8 mushrooms, chopped
1 medium onion, finely chopped
2 garlic cloves, minced
1 cup breadcrumbs

4 veal cutlets, pounded thin
1 tsp. olive oil
¼ cup shredded mozzarella cheese
4 tbs. dry sherry
6 mushrooms, sliced

Melt butter in a skillet. Add chopped mushrooms, onion and garlic and sauté for 5 minutes. Add ½ cup breadcrumbs and mix. Spread an equal amount of stuffing in center of each piece of veal and roll tightly. Secure with wooden picks. Coat veal rolls in remaining ½ cup breadcrumbs. Lay out two 18-x-15-inch sheets of parchment paper and fold in half. Brush inside of paper with olive oil. Place 2 veal rolls on one side of each sheet. Do not let veal overlap. Sprinkle each roll with cheese and drizzle with sherry. Surround with sliced mushrooms. Fold and tightly seal each packet. Place packets on a baking sheet and bake in a preheated 375° oven for 25 minutes.

BAKED CHUCK ROAST

Servings: 6

It's almost cheating to use prepared foods — the mushroom soup-onion soup mix combination makes this not only quick to prepare, but very tasty.

4 lb. boneless chuck roast
1 can (10¾ oz.) cream of mushroom soup
1 envelope dehydrated onion soup mix
¼ tsp. freshly ground pepper
¼ tsp. dried thyme

Lay a 15-x-25-inch sheet of parchment paper inside a roasting pan. Place chuck roast on top of parchment paper. In a medium bowl, combine all remaining ingredients and spread over roast. Tightly wrap roast with parchment paper. Roast in a preheated 325° oven for 2½ hours. Pour liquid in a sauce boat and pass it to your guests.

LEG OF LAMB
Servings: 6

The flavorful juices from this recipe should be used as a sauce or gravy.

6 lb. leg of lamb
½ tbs. olive oil
1 large garlic clove, cut in half
¼ tsp. dried rosemary
¼ tsp. dried dill weed
freshly ground pepper
4-6 tarragon sprigs

Brush lamb with oil and rub with garlic. Sprinkle with rosemary, dill weed and pepper. Wrap lamb tightly in parchment paper. Place in a large roasting pan. Bake in a preheated oven at 350° for 1½ hours or until a meat thermometer reads 165°. Remove lamb from oven and let sit for 10 minutes before carving. Garnish with tarragon sprigs. Pour the liquid into a sauce boat and pass it to your guests.

LAMB WITH SUN-DRIED TOMATOES

Servings: 4

The sun-dried tomatoes add zest and go well with lamb.

1 medium onion, chopped
3 tbs. vinegar
2 tbs. honey
¾ cup white wine
½ cup chopped sun-dried tomatoes, reconstituted or marinated
¼ tsp. freshly ground pepper
4 lb. lamb shanks, or lamb riblets
1 medium green bell pepper, chopped

In a small bowl, combine all ingredients except lamb and bell pepper. Quickly brown lamb in a heated skillet. Trim off fat and discard drippings. Place lamb in a parchment- lined casserole. Pour mixture over lamb. Scatter chopped green pepper over lamb. Cover with a sheet of parchment paper. Bake in a preheated 325° oven for 1½ hours. Serve lamb directly from casserole.

LAMB KABOBS
Servings: 3

The parchment paper prevents the lamb from drying out while it cooks.

1 lb. lean lamb
2 tbs. olive oil
1 medium onion
18 cherry tomatoes
18 mushroom caps

2 tbs. lemon juice
1/8 tsp. dried thyme
1/8 tsp. dried rosemary
1/8 tsp. freshly ground pepper

Cut lamb into 1-inch cubes. Heat 1 tbs. olive oil in a skillet and brown lamb for 2 minutes. Cut onion into quarters and separate layers. Alternately thread lamb, tomatoes, onion and mushroom caps onto 6 bamboo skewers. Lay out three 18-x-15-inch sheets of parchment paper or three parchment hearts and fold. Unfold paper and place two skewers on one side of each sheet next to fold. Leave 1 inch between skewers. Drizzle with 1 tbs. olive oil and lemon juice. Season with thyme, rosemary and pepper. Fold and tightly seal packets. Place packets on a baking sheet in a preheated oven at 375° for 30 minutes.

LAMB CHOPS WITH STEWED TOMATOES

Servings: 2

This is great served with white rice.

1 tbs. butter
2 garlic cloves, minced
⅛ tsp. freshly ground pepper
2 lamb chops

1 can (14.5 oz.) stewed tomatoes
½ medium onion, thinly sliced
¼ tsp. ground cloves
½ tsp. dried oregano

Melt butter in a skillet over medium heat. Add garlic and pepper and sauté lamb for 2 minutes on each side. Set aside. Drain liquid from tomatoes and discard. Lay out a 15-x-20-inch sheet of parchment paper and fold in half. Unfold paper and place chops next to fold. Do not let chops overlap. Spread tomatoes and onion over chops. Season with cloves and oregano. Drizzle with melted butter mixture from skillet. Fold and tightly seal packet. Place on a baking sheet and bake in a preheated 375° oven for 30 minutes.

CROWN ROAST OF LAMB
Servings: 6

Ask your butcher for a crown roast of 2 racks of lamb, tied back to back, forming a circle. For easy carving, bones between ribs should be cracked. The lamb browns nicely and bakes in its own natural juices. This is a wonderful dish for special occasions and holidays. Dress it up with parchment frills and wow your guests.

2 lb. crown roast of lamb
Stuffing for Crown Roast of Lamb, follows
2 tbs. olive oil
1/8 tsp. dried thyme
1/8 tsp. dried rosemary
pepper to season

Set roast upright in a large shallow roasting pan lined with parchment paper. Press *Stuffing for Crown Roast of Lamb* into cavity of roast. Combine oil, thyme and rosemary. Brush roast with mixture and season with pepper. Wrap roast tightly in parchment paper. Place in a preheated 350° oven for 1 1/2 hours. Before serving, place a parchment frill over each bone (see page 9).

STUFFING FOR CROWN ROAST OF LAMB

4 tbs. butter
1 medium onion, finely chopped
1/4 cup finely chopped mushrooms
1/2 tsp. crushed mint
pepper to taste
1 cup breadcrumbs

Melt butter in a skillet over medium heat. Add onion, mushrooms, mint and pepper. Sauté for 3 to 4 minutes. Add breadcrumbs and mix.

LAMB CHOPS WITH LEMON AND MINT
Servings: 4

Serve chops in packets for a stunning and impressive presentation.

2 tbs. olive oil
4 lamb chops
1 medium carrot, thinly sliced
1 medium onion, thinly sliced
2 stalks celery, thinly sliced
1 garlic clove, minced

1/8 tsp. dried oregano
1/8 tsp. dried rosemary
8 lemon slices
1/8 tsp. pepper
1/2 tsp. dried mint

Heat 1 tbs. olive oil in a skillet; sauté lamb for 2 minutes on each side over medium heat. Remove from skillet and set aside. Heat 1 tbs. oil in skillet; sauté carrot, onion, celery, garlic, oregano and rosemary for 3 minutes. Lay out four 18-x-15-inch sheets of parchment paper and fold in half. Unfold paper and place 1 chop next to fold on each sheet. Divide vegetables equally over and around each chop. Top with lemon slices; season with pepper and mint. Fold and tightly seal each packet. Place packets on a baking sheet and bake in a preheated 375° oven for 30 minutes. Transfer packets to individual serving plates, allowing guests to open packets at the table.

BEEF AND EGGPLANT CASSEROLE

Servings: 4

This dish is simple to prepare and really delicious. Check the eggplant for ripeness. It should be fresh and firm — not too soft or hard.

1 lb. lean ground beef
¼ cup chopped celery
2 medium onions, chopped
1 garlic clove, minced
1 tsp. basil, dried

½ tsp. dried chervil
¼ freshly ground pepper
1 eggplant
1½ cups tomato sauce

Quickly brown beef in a nonstick skillet. Drain off fat and place beef in a large bowl. Combine with celery, onion, garlic, basil, chervil and pepper. Peel and cut eggplant lengthwise into ⅛-inch slices. In a parchment-lined casserole, arrange a layer of eggplant slices. Cover with meat mixture; repeat process ending with a layer of eggplant. Spread tomato sauce on top. Place casserole in a preheated 350° oven for 50 minutes. Reduce heat to 325° and bake for 20 more minutes.

BEEF FRANKFURTERS AND BEANS
Servings: 4

Serve this old favorite with brown bread.

4 beef frankfurters
1 can (28 oz.) baked beans
1 medium onion, diced
2 tbs. molasses
⅓ cup brown sugar
3 strips uncooked bacon

Cut frankfurters into ¼-inch slices. Combine all ingredients except bacon in a bowl and mix. Line an 8-x-11-inch casserole with a large sheet of parchment paper. Leave extra paper on sides to fold over and cover casserole. Spread mixture in casserole. Lay bacon on top and cover with paper. Place in a preheated 350° oven for 30 minutes. Fold open parchment paper cover; raise temperature to 450° and bake for 15 more minutes.

FABULOUS MEATBALLS

Servings: 6

This can be served over fresh fettucine or as an appetizer.

1 lb. ground chuck
½ cup crushed tomatoes
2 medium onions, minced
¼ cup bulghur wheat
1 garlic clove, minced
¼ tsp. dried basil

¼ tsp. dried oregano
¼ tsp. freshly ground pepper
¾ cup breadcrumbs
2 cups fresh spinach, trimmed,
  stemmed
1 cup tomato sauce

In a large bowl, combine beef, tomatoes, onions, bulghur, garlic, basil, oregano, pepper and breadcrumbs. Using hands, mix thoroughly. Form into 30 meatballs, about 1½ inches in diameter. Line an ovenproof casserole with parchment paper. Place a bed of spinach in casserole. Arrange meatballs on spinach and top with tomato sauce. Cover casserole with a sheet of parchment paper. Place in a preheated 325° oven for 1 hour. Remove top sheet of paper and bake for 15 more minutes.

STUFFED ROLLED FLANK STEAK
Servings: 6

The tender beef surrounds a delicious savory stuffing for a wonderful presentation.

2 lb. flank steak
2 cups breadcrumbs
6 tbs. chopped celery
1 medium onion, minced
1 garlic clove, minced
1/2 tsp. Dijon mustard
1/4 tsp. ground sage

1/8 tsp. dried basil
1/8 tsp. dried thyme
1/4 tsp. freshly ground pepper
3/4 cup water
2 tbs. butter, melted
1 tbs. olive oil
1/8 tsp. dried rosemary

Pound steak with a meat mallet to tenderize. Cut into 2 large pieces. Rinse and pat dry. In a medium bowl, combine breadcrumbs, celery, onion, garlic, mustard, sage, basil, thyme, 1/8 tsp. pepper, water and butter. Spoon stuffing over both pieces of meat. Roll and tie with butcher's twine or picks. Heat oil in a skillet. Quickly brown all sides of rolled beef. Sprinkle with rosemary and remaining pepper. Wrap each rolled flank steak in a 22-x-15-inch sheet of parchment paper. Place on a baking sheet and bake in a preheated 325° oven for 50 minutes. Unwrap and transfer to a large platter.

SAVORY BEEF BAKE

Servings: 1

This can be served plain or with a spicy tomato sauce.

½ cup cubed flank steak
1 cup cubed pork steak
1 cup thinly sliced potatoes
½ cup thinly sliced carrots
2 tbs. minced onion
½ tsp. dried parsley
¼ tsp. dried basil
¼ tsp. freshly ground pepper
1 tsp. butter

In a bowl, combine all ingredients except butter. Lay out an 18-x-15-inch sheet of parchment paper and fold in half. Unfold sheet and place mixture on one side of paper next to fold. Dot with butter. Fold and tightly seal packet. Place packet on a baking sheet in a preheated 425° oven for 20 minutes. Reduce temperature to 325° and bake for 30 minutes more.

BEEF CURRY
Servings: 4

Serve this delicious curry with steamed white rice.

2 lb. rump or top round boneless beef
1 cup flour
3 tbs. butter
1/4 cup olive oil
1 garlic clove, minced
1 tsp. ground ginger

3 cups minced onions
1 tbs. mild curry powder
1 medium Granny Smith apple, peeled,
　cored, diced
1 tsp. cumin
1/2 tsp. cardamom

Cut beef into 1½-inch cubes and dredge in flour. Heat 2 tbs. butter and oil in a large sauté pan. Add beef and sauté until brown. Remove from pan and set aside. Melt 1 tbs. butter in sauté pan. Add garlic, ginger, onions and curry. Sauté for 3 minutes. Add apple and sauté for 2 minutes. In a large bowl, combine apple-onion mixture, beef, cumin and cardamom. Mix thoroughly. Lay out four 18-x-15-inch sheets of parchment paper and fold in half. Unfold sheets and place 1/4 beef mixture on one side of each sheet next to fold. Fold and seal tightly. Place packets on baking sheets and bake in a preheated 325° oven for 50 minutes. Transfer packets to individual serving plates, allowing guests to open packets at the table.

RIO GRANDE MEAT LOAF

Servings: 6

This change-of-pace meat loaf has a spicy southwestern flavor.

2 cups breadcrumbs
2 lb. ground beef
2 eggs, beaten
2 medium onions, minced
1¾ cups crushed tomatoes
1 tsp. jalapeño pepper flakes
¼ tsp. dried red pepper flakes

In a large bowl, combine breadcrumbs, ground beef, eggs, onions, ¾ cup tomatoes and jalapeño flakes. Using hands, mix thoroughly. Line a 9-x-4-x-3 inch loaf pan with parchment paper. Allow paper to extend 2 inches above sides to prevent food from running over. Pat beef mixture evenly into pan. Spoon remaining 1 cup tomatoes over meat loaf. Sprinkle with crushed red pepper. Bake in a preheated 350° oven until done, about 1½ hours.

BEEF WITH RED WINE
Servings: 4

This is great with a fresh garden salad.

2 lb. rump or top round boneless beef
1 cup flour
1/4 cup olive oil
2 tbs. butter
1 garlic clove, minced
2 cups diagonally sliced celery

2 large onions, chopped
1/4 tsp. dried thyme
1/4 tsp. dried oregano
1/4 tsp. freshly ground pepper
1 tbs. red wine

Rinse beef and pat dry. Cut into 1½-inch cubes. Dredge beef in flour. Heat oil and butter in a large sauté pan. Sauté garlic for 30 seconds. Add beef and sauté until brown. In a large bowl, combine beef with celery, onions, thyme, oregano, pepper and wine. Mix thoroughly. Lay out four 18-x-15-inch sheets of parchment paper and fold in half. Unfold sheets and place 1/4 meat mixture on one side of each sheet next to fold. Fold and seal tightly. Place packets on baking sheets in a preheated 325° oven for 1 hour. Transfer packets to individual serving plates.

CANTONESE GINGER BEEF WITH BROCCOLI

Servings: 4

You can substitute sirloin or chuck steak for the flank steak. Serve this over steamed white rice.

1 tbs. cornstarch
2 tbs. light soy sauce
1 tbs. sherry
1 garlic clove, minced
1 tsp. ground ginger
½ tsp. sugar

1 lb. beef flank steak
2 tbs. vegetable oil
1 medium red or green bell pepper
1 medium onion
4 cups (1 medium bunch) 1-inch
   broccoli florettes

Combine cornstarch, soy sauce, sherry, garlic, ginger and sugar in a large bowl and mix thoroughly. Set aside. Rinse beef and pat dry. Thinly slice beef across grain into 2-x-¼-inch-thick pieces and marinate for 30 minutes. Heat oil in a sauté pan. Quickly sauté beef until brown, about 2 minutes. Slice pepper into matchstick strips. Cut onion into ¼-inch slices. Combine beef with pepper, onion and broccoli. Lay out two 18-x-15-inch sheets of parchment paper and fold in half. Unfold sheets. Place half of mixture on one side of each sheet next to fold. Do not overlap beef. Fold and tightly seal packets. Place on a baking sheet and bake in a preheated 325° oven for 25 minutes.

SIRLOIN TIP KABOBS
Servings: 6

This is delicious served over long-grain white rice.

1½ lb. sirloin tips
¼ cup extra virgin olive oil
¼ cup soy sauce
¼ cup dry sherry
2 tbs. minced onion
½ tsp. sesame oil
1 tsp. minced cilantro

½ tsp. orange zest
1 garlic clove, minced
½ tsp. minced fresh ginger root
2 medium zucchini
2 medium onions
18 cherry tomatoes

Cut sirloin into 1½-inch pieces. In a large bowl, combine beef, oil, soy sauce, sherry, onion, sesame oil, cilantro, orange zest, garlic and ginger root. Marinate for 2 hours. Cut zucchini into 1-inch chunks and onions into 1-inch slices. Alternately thread beef, zucchini, tomato and onion slices onto 6 bamboo skewers. Lay out three 18-x-15-inch sheets of parchment paper and fold in half. Unfold sheets and place 2 beef skewers on one side of each sheet next to fold. Fold and seal tightly. Place packets on a baking sheet and bake in a preheated 325° oven for 25 minutes.

FISH AND SHELLFISH

SKEWERED SHRIMP AND FRESH SPINACH

Servings: 4

This recipe can be easily adapted for larger or smaller servings.

2 medium onions
2 green, yellow or red bell peppers
4 cups fresh spinach, trimmed,
  stemmed
2 dozen large shrimp, shelled, deveined

2 dozen cherry tomatoes
4 garlic cloves, crushed
1 tsp. chopped fresh parsley
white ground pepper to taste
4 tbs. dry sherry

Cut onions into quarters and separate layers. Cut peppers into 1-inch pieces. Lay out four 18-x-15-inch sheets of parchment paper and fold in half. Unfold sheets and spread equal amounts of spinach on one side of each sheet next to fold. Alternately thread shrimp, tomatoes, peppers and onions onto bamboo skewers. Lay 2 skewers over each bed of spinach. Do not overlap skewers. Top each skewer with crushed garlic, parsley and white pepper. Drizzle with dry sherry. Fold and tightly seal each packet. Place packets on baking sheets and bake in a preheated 375° oven for 20 minutes. Transfer packets to individual serving plates, allowing guests to open packets at the table.

STUFFED SALMON

Servings: 4

*This dish goes well with **Hollandaise Sauce**, page 137. Serve with potatoes and a crisp green salad.*

4 whole salmon, boned, dressed,
  1 lb. each
2 tbs. butter
1/2 cup chopped fresh parsley

1/2 cup chopped fresh chives
1/4 cup chopped onion
2 tbs. lemon juice
8 slices lemon, thinly cut

Rinse salmon under cold water and pat dry. To make stuffing, melt butter and mix with parsley, chives, onion and lemon juice. Stuff each fish cavity with 1/4 of the stuffing and 2 slices of lemon. Lay out four 18-x-15-inch sheets of parchment paper or 4 parchment hearts and fold in half. Unfold parchment sheets and place 1 stuffed fish on one side of each sheet next to fold. Fold and tightly seal each packet. Place packets on baking sheets and bake in a preheated 375° oven for 15 minutes. Transfer packets to individual serving plates, allowing guests to open packets at the table.

LEMON PEPPER SCALLOPS
Servings: 4

This parchment-wrapped dish goes directly from the oven to the table.

1 lb. whole bay scallops, or sea scallops,
  cut into thirds
1 cup shredded carrots
1/2 cup chopped scallions

4 tbs. lemon juice
1/4 tsp. dried parsley
1/4 tsp. freshly ground white pepper
2 tbs. butter

Rinse scallops under cold water. To release liquid from scallops, place in a dry nonstick skillet set on low heat. Raise heat setting to medium and cook for 2 minutes. Remove scallops from pan and drain. Lay out four 18-x-15-inch sheets of parchment paper or 4 parchment hearts and fold in half. Unfold parchment and place equal amounts of carrots and scallions on one side of each sheet next to fold. Divide scallops equally over carrots and scallions. Do not let scallops overlap. Drizzle with lemon juice, season with parsley and pepper, and dot with butter. Fold and tightly seal each packet. Place packets on baking sheets and bake in a preheated 400° oven for 10 minutes. Transfer packets to individual serving plates, allowing guests to open packets at the table.

HERB BAKED SCALLOPS

Servings: 4

The ideal cooking method for scallops is in parchment paper packets.

1 lb. whole bay scallops, or sea scallops, cut into thirds
1 tbs. olive oil
1 garlic clove, minced
1 cup chopped tomatoes

½ cup chopped onion
1 cup whole button mushrooms
¼ tsp. dried basil
½ tsp. dried parsley
2 tbs. butter

Rinse scallops under cold water. To release liquid from scallops, place in a dry nonstick skillet set on low heat. Raise heat setting to medium and cook for 2 minutes. Remove scallops from pan and drain. Heat oil in skillet and sauté garlic, tomatoes, onion, mushrooms and basil for 3 minutes. Lay out four 18-x-15-inch sheets of parchment paper or 4 parchment hearts and fold. Unfold parchment sheets. Distribute equal amounts of vegetables on one side of each sheet next to fold. Cover vegetables with equal amounts of scallops. Do not let scallops overlap. Cover scallops with remaining vegetables. Sprinkle with parsley and dot with butter. Fold and tightly seal each packet. Place packets on baking sheets and bake in a preheated 400° oven for 10 minutes. Let guests open packets at the table.

BASS WITH FIVE PEPPERCORN BLEND
Servings: 4

Enjoy the taste and aroma of freshly ground gourmet peppercorns with fresh fish. Five blend peppercorn spice is available at most gourmet shops or you can make your own with the recipe on the next page.

4 bass fillets, 6 oz. each
1/2 cup chopped celery
1/2 cup shredded carrots
1/4 cup chopped scallions
juice of 1 lemon
1/2 tsp. fennel
1 tsp. freshly ground five peppercorn blend, follows
2 tbs. butter

Rinse fish under cold water and pat dry. Combine celery, carrots, scallions, lemon juice, fennel and five peppercorn blend in a bowl and mix. Lay out four 18-x-15-inch sheets of parchment paper and fold in half. Unfold parchment sheets. Using half of vegetables, place equal amounts on one side of each sheet next to fold. Place 1 fillet over each bed of vegetables and top with remaining vegetables. Dot with butter. Fold and tightly seal each packet. Place packets on baking sheets and bake in a preheated 375° oven for 20 minutes. Transfer packets to individual serving plates, allowing guests to open packets at the table.

FIVE PEPPERCORN BLEND

2 tbs. whole black Tellecherry peppercorns
2 tbs. whole black malabar peppercorns
2 tbs. whole white montok peppercorns
2 tbs. whole green Brazilian peppercorns
2 tbs. whole baises roses peppercorns

Mix peppercorns together and grind just before using.

BAKED SALMON
Servings: 4

Salmon, wrapped in parchment paper and cooked in its own distinctively flavored juices with cream cheese and fresh vegetables, becomes a delicious, delightful dish.

4 salmon steaks, 6-8 oz. each
4 oz. cream cheese
1 medium-sized firm tomato, peeled, chopped
½ cup thinly sliced mushrooms
½ cup chopped fresh chives
2 tbs. chopped fresh basil
2 tbs. chopped fresh parsley
1 tsp. freshly ground pepper
1 tbs. olive oil
2 tbs. grated Parmesan cheese
2 tbs. lemon juice
cilantro or basil sprigs for garnish
8 lemon wedges

Rinse fish under cold water and pat dry. In a large bowl, combine cream cheese, tomato, mushrooms, chives, basil, parsley and pepper. Lay out four 18-x-15-inch sheets of parchment paper or 4 hearts and brush entire surface with oil. Fold sheets in half so oiled sides are facing each other. Unfold parchment sheets and sprinkle 1 side of each sheet with Parmesan cheese. Place 1 salmon steak on top of cheese next to fold. Spread equal portions of cream cheese mixture on each piece of salmon. Drizzle with lemon juice. Fold and tightly seal each packet. Place packets on baking sheets and bake in a preheated 400° oven for 20 minutes. Transfer packets to individual serving plates. Garnish with cilantro or basil sprigs and serve with lemon wedges.

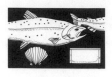

PASTA WITH CLAMS AND VEGETABLES
Servings: 4

The pasta is wrapped in parchment paper, absorbing the subtle flavor of the clams and vegetables.

2 lb. small clams in shells
salt
½ tsp. oatmeal
1 bay leaf
8 oz. dried angel hair pasta
1 tbs. olive oil
1 garlic clove, crushed
1 large onion, finely chopped
2 medium tomatoes, diced
1 tsp. dried thyme
½ tsp. freshly ground pepper
1 cup white wine
2 cups water
2 tbs. butter
4 tbs. grated Parmesan cheese

Be sure all clam shells are closed tightly. Tap shells that are open to see if they will close. Discard all that don't close. Scrub clams under cold running water with a stiff brush. Place in a large pan of cold salted water with oatmeal for 20 minutes. Clams feed on oatmeal and will discharge their sand. Rinse again in cold salted water. Place in a covered saucepan with ½ cup water and 1 bay leaf. Cook for 4 to 5 minutes over high heat until shells open. Discard clams that have not opened after cooking. Remove clams from shells, Rinse in hot water and chop into small pieces.

Partially cook angel hair pasta until limp, about 2 minutes in boiling water. Rinse under cold water. Drain and set aside.

Heat oil in a skillet and sauté garlic, onion, tomatoes, thyme and pepper for 5 minutes. Lay out four 18-x-15-inch sheets of parchment paper and fold in half. Unfold parchment sheets and place ¼ of the pasta on one side of each sheet next to fold. Arrange equal portions of sautéed vegetables and chopped clams on top of pasta. Drizzle each packet with ¼ cup wine and ½ cup water. Dot with butter and sprinkle with Parmesan cheese. Fold and tightly seal each packet. Place packets on baking sheets and bake in a preheated 350° oven for 12 minutes. Transfer packets to individual serving plates. Serve immediately.

POLLOCK WITH SPINACH
Servings: 4

This recipe works equally well with cod or haddock.

2 lb. pollock fillets
½ lb. fresh spinach, trimmed, stemmed
4 tbs. dry white wine
1 tbs. lemon juice
¼ tsp. pepper
2 tbs. butter
4 tbs. grated Parmesan cheese

Cut fish into 4 equal pieces. Rinse under cold water and pat dry. Lay out four 18-x-15-inch sheets of parchment paper and fold in half. Unfold sheets and spread equal amounts of spinach on one side of each sheet next to fold. Place fish on top of spinach and cover with white wine, lemon juice and pepper. Dot with butter and sprinkle with cheese. Fold and tightly seal each packet. Place packets on baking sheets and bake in a preheated 400° oven for 15 minutes. Transfer packets to individual serving plates, allowing guests to open packets at the table.

OVEN FRIED CATFISH

Servings: 2

This is a quick and easy way to prepare fresh fish. It makes a delicious casual dinner.

1 lb. fish fillets — catfish, hake, haddock or cod
½ cup Italian salad dressing
½ cup breadcrumbs
4 lemon wedges

Rinse fillets under cold water and pat dry. Marinate fillets in dressing and refrigerate for 20 to 30 minutes. Coat with breadcrumbs and shake off excess. Place fillets on a parchment-lined baking sheet. Do not let fillets overlap. Bake in a preheated 450° oven for 12 minutes. Serve with lemon wedges.

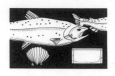

ITALIAN-STYLE COD
Servings: 4

This is a super time-saver. Simply wrap the ingredients and bake. It's delicious yet effortless.

2 lb. cod fillets
1 jar (15 oz.) meatless spaghetti sauce, or tomato sauce
1 cup shredded mozzarella cheese
salt and pepper to taste
¼ tsp. oregano

Cut fish into 4 equal pieces. Rinse under cold water and pat dry. Lay out four 18-x-15-inch sheets of parchment paper and fold. Unfold sheets and place equal amounts of fish on one side of each sheet next to fold. Spread sauce over fish, covering fillets. Top with cheese, salt, pepper and oregano. Fold and tightly seal each packet. Place packets on baking sheets and bake in a preheated 400° oven for 25 minutes. Carefully transfer packets to individual serving plates, allowing guests to open packets at the table.

QUICK BAKED COD

Servings: 4

Packets can be prepared up to 24 hours in advance. Be sure to store them in the coldest part of the refrigerator.

2 lb. cod fillets
2 tbs. butter, melted
2/3 cup breadcrumbs
1/2 tsp. garlic powder

1/2 tsp. onion powder
juice of 1 lemon
1/4 tsp. dried basil
freshly ground pepper to taste

Cut fish into 4 equal pieces. Rinse under cold water and pat dry. Coat fish with butter. In a shallow dish, combine breadcrumbs, garlic powder and onion powder. Coat fish in mixture and shake off excess. Lay out four 18-x-15-inch sheets of parchment paper and fold. Unfold paper and place equal amounts of cod on one side of each sheet next to fold. Sprinkle with lemon juice and season with basil and pepper. Fold and tightly seal each packet. Place packets on baking sheets and bake in a preheated 400° oven for 20 minutes. Transfer packets to individual serving plates, allowing guests to open packets at the table.

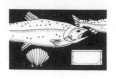

SWORDFISH KABOBS WITH BALSAMIC VINAIGRETTE
Servings: 4

Be sure to purchase a top quality balsamic vinegar. Look for the seal of authenticity.

1 lb. swordfish
2 tbs. balsamic vinegar
¼ tsp. black pepper
1 garlic clove, minced

½ cup extra virgin olive oil
2 medium onions
16 cherry tomatoes
¼ cup finely chopped fresh parsley

Rinse fish under cold water, pat dry and cut into 1½-inch pieces. To make vinaigrette, combine vinegar, pepper, garlic and olive oil in a small bowl and blend well. Combine fish with vinaigrette and marinate in the refrigerator for 1 hour. Cut onions into quarters and separate layers. Alternately thread swordfish cubes, tomatoes and onions onto bamboo skewers. Lay out four 18-x-15-inch sheets of parchment paper and fold in half. Unfold paper and lay 2 skewers on one side of each sheet next to fold. Drizzle remaining vinaigrette over skewers and sprinkle with parsley. Fold and tightly seal each packet. Place packets on baking sheets and bake in a preheated 375° oven for 20 minutes. Allow guests to open packets at the table.

PARCHMENT HALIBUT

Servings: 4

This is a wonderful dish to serve in individual packets. Your guests will find it interesting and delicious. Serve with fresh steamed seasonal vegetables.

four 1-inch thick halibut steaks, 8 oz.
  each
1 tsp. minced fresh parsley
4 garlic cloves, crushed

1 tsp. minced fresh ginger root
4 tbs. fresh lemon juice
1 tsp. extra virgin olive oil
freshly ground pepper

Rinse fish under cold water and pat dry. In a small bowl, combine parsley, garlic, ginger root and lemon juice. Lay out four 18-x-15-inch sheets of parchment paper or 4 hearts and fold in half. Brush both sides of fish with olive oil. Unfold paper and lay halibut on one side of each sheet next to fold. Pour an equal amount of lemon mixture over each piece of fish. Season with pepper. Fold and tightly seal each packet. Place packets on baking sheets and bake in a preheated 475° oven for 20 minutes. Transfer packets to individual plates, allowing guests to open packets at the table.

STUFFED SOLE
Servings: 4

A fillet of perch or flounder will substitute nicely.

2 lb. sole fillets
1 tbs. lemon juice
¼ tsp. dried basil
freshly ground pepper to taste
2 tbs. butter
Stuffing, follows

Cut sole fillets into 4 equal pieces. Rinse fillets under cold water and pat dry. Lay out four 18-x-15-inch sheets of parchment paper and fold in half. Unfold paper and place 1 fillet on one side of each sheet next to fold. Divide stuffing evenly and spread over each fillet. Roll and fasten with wooden picks. Pour lemon juice over fish. Season with basil and pepper and dot with butter. Fold and tightly seal each packet. Place packets on baking sheets and bake in a preheated 375° oven for 25 minutes. Carefully transfer packets to serving plates and allow guests to open them at the table.

STUFFING

¼ cup butter
½ cup diced celery
⅓ cup diced onion
1 garlic clove, minced
freshly ground pepper to taste
1¼ cups breadcrumbs
2 tbs. water
½ lb. shrimp, shelled, deveined, chopped

Melt butter in a large skillet. Combine celery, onion, garlic and pepper and sauté for 3 to 4 minutes. Stir in breadcrumbs, water and shrimp. Mix thoroughly.

SWORDFISH WITH DILL WEED
Servings: 4

This is a quick and easy method to prepare swordfish. The vegetables, cut into julienne, or matchstick strips, always seem to give food a more attractive appearance.

2 swordfish steaks, 8 oz. each
2 tbs. olive oil
juice of 1 lemon
1 tsp. dried dill weed

2 medium carrots, cut into matchstick strips
1 medium zucchini, cut into matchstick strips

Rinse fish under cold water and pat dry. To prepare marinade, combine olive oil, lemon juice and dill weed in a large shallow dish. Place fish in marinade, coating each side. Refrigerate for 2 hours. Lay out two 18-x-15-inch sheets of parchment paper or 2 hearts and fold in half. Unfold paper and scatter half of carrots and zucchini on one side of each sheet. Place swordfish steaks on top of vegetables. Arrange remaining vegetables over fish. Fold and tightly seal each packet. Place packets on baking sheets and bake in a preheated 375° oven for 20 minutes. Transfer packets to individual serving plates.

LEMON GARLIC SHRIMP

Servings: 2

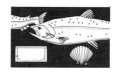

If shrimp have been frozen, it is important to drain off excess liquid. Place them in a colander and refrigerate for 2 hours to drain. This dish is great served over linguine.

1 lb. large shrimp, shelled, deveined
1 cup tomatoes, diced
6 garlic cloves, crushed
1½ cups sliced mushrooms

¼ cup diced scallions
2 tbs. lemon juice
4 tbs. butter
½ tsp. chopped fresh parsley

In a large bowl, combine all ingredients except butter and parsley. Mix and refrigerate for 4 hours or overnight. Lay out two 18-x-15-inch sheets of parchment paper and fold in half. Unfold paper and place half of shrimp mixture on one side of each sheet of paper. Do not let shrimp overlap. Dot with butter and sprinkle with parsley. Fold and tightly seal each packet. Place packets on baking sheets and bake in a preheated 375° oven for 20 minutes.

BAKED TUNA
Servings: 4

Look for fresh yellowfin or bluefin tuna. This recipe also works with swordfish or shark.

2 lb. tuna steaks
1 tbs. olive oil
1 garlic clove, crushed
1 medium onion, thinly sliced
1 medium tomato, chopped
1 large carrot, thinly sliced

$\frac{1}{8}$ tsp. freshly ground pepper
$\frac{1}{2}$ cup white wine
$\frac{1}{2}$ tsp. dried basil
$\frac{1}{4}$ tsp. ground rosemary
8 lemon wedges

Rinse fish under cold water. Heat oil in a skillet. Sauté garlic and onion for 3 minutes. Add tomato and carrot and sauté for another 3 minutes. Line a 12-x-12-inch ovenproof casserole with parchment paper. Place fish in casserole and sprinkle with pepper. Cover with sautéed vegetables and drizzle with white wine. Sprinkle with basil and rosemary. Bake casserole in a preheated 425° oven for 15 minutes. Serve with lemon wedges.

CATFISH CASSEROLE

Servings: 4

This is a delicious treatment for catfish, and it's easy cleanup, too.

2 lb. catfish fillets
1 medium carrot, diced
1 medium onion, thinly sliced
1 medium zucchini, thinly sliced
½ cup white wine

¼ tsp. dried marjoram
¼ tsp. dried basil
1 cup sour cream
½ tsp. Dijon mustard
¼ tsp. chopped fresh chives

Rinse catfish under cold water. Line a 12-x-12-inch ovenproof casserole with parchment paper. Place a layer of carrot, onion and zucchini in casserole. Arrange a single layer of fish fillets on top of vegetables. Slowly pour wine over fish and sprinkle with marjoram and basil. Cover casserole with parchment paper and bake for 20 to 25 minutes in a preheated 400° oven. Combine sour cream with mustard and chives. Remove parchment cover from casserole and spread sour cream mixture over fish. Broil for 4 minutes.

PESTO SWORDFISH OVER LENTILS
Servings: 4

Wonderful aromas are trapped inside the parchment packets.

1 cup lentils
2 qt. water
2 cups fresh basil leaves
3 garlic cloves
1 cup olive oil

½ cup pine nuts or chopped walnuts
¼ tsp. freshly ground pepper
½ cup grated Parmesan cheese
4 swordfish steaks, about 2 lb. total
1 medium tomato, diced

Rinse lentils under cold water. Bring lentils to a boil in water. Reduce heat and simmer for 40 minutes. To make pesto, combine basil, garlic, olive oil, nuts, and pepper in a blender or food processor. Puree for 15 to 20 seconds, until a paste forms. Pour into a bowl and mix in grated cheese. Lay out four 18-x-15 sheets of parchment paper or 4 parchment hearts and fold in half. Drain lentils. Unfold paper and place ¼ of the lentils on one side of each sheet next to fold. Rinse fish under cold water. Place 1 swordfish steak on each bed of lentils. Cover with a layer of pesto and top with diced tomatoes. Fold and tightly seal each packet. Place packets on baking sheets and bake in a preheated 400° oven for 20 minutes.

TARRAGON AND PARSLEY SCROD

Servings: 4

Scrod is a term for a 1½ to 2½ lb. cod, cusk, haddock, hake, pollock or tomcod.

2 lb. cod fillets
4 tbs. butter
2 tbs. lemon juice
½ cup chopped fresh parsley
¼ tsp. dried tarragon
1 tsp. grated Parmesan cheese

½ tsp. dried basil
1½ cups breadcrumbs
1 tsp. olive oil
freshly ground pepper to taste
8 lemon wedges
8 cilantro sprigs

Cut fish into 4 equal pieces and rinse under cold water. Melt butter in a skillet and stir in breadcrumbs. Add parsley, tarragon, basil, cheese, lemon juice and pepper. Blend well and set aside. Lay out four 18-x-15-inch sheets of parchment paper and fold in half. Unfold paper and brush inside with oil. Place ¼ fish on one side of each sheet next to fold. Cover fish with a layer of breadcrumb mixture. Fold and tightly seal packets. Place packets on a baking sheet and bake in a preheated 375° oven for 25 minutes. Transfer packets to serving plates garnished with cilantro sprigs and lemon wedges. Let guests open packets at the table.

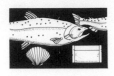

POACHED HALIBUT
Servings: 4

A tantalizing mixture of spices flavor this poached fish dish. The parchment packets go directly into the boiling water.

1 lb. halibut
2 qt. water
1 onion, sliced
½ carrot, sliced
¼ tsp. chopped fresh parsley
1 bay leaf
5 whole peppercorns
5 whole cloves
¼ tsp. fennel seed
1 tsp. vinegar
4 cilantro sprigs
4 lemon wedges

Rinse fish under cold water. Bring water to a boil in a 3-quart sauté pan. Add onion, carrot, parsley, bay leaf, peppercorns, cloves, fennel and vinegar to water, reduce heat and simmer for 5 minutes. Lay out two 18-x-15-inch sheets of parchment paper and fold in half. Unfold paper and place half of fish in center of each sheet. Fold paper packets with a secure wrap for poaching (see page 4). Lower packets into sauté pan and simmer for 5 minutes. Turn packets over and simmer for 5 more minutes. Remove packets from pan and transfer to individual serving plates. Garnish with fresh cilantro sprigs and lemon wedges. Serve plain or with *Hollandaise Sauce*.

HOLLANDAISE SAUCE

3 egg yolks, at room temperature
2 tbs. water, at room temperature
2 tsp. lemon juice

6 oz. butter
1/8 tsp. paprika

Over low heat, whip egg yolks, water and lemon juice in a double boiler until creamy. Cut butter into 1/2-inch slices and add to sauce, 1 piece at a time, allowing butter to slowly melt in sauce each time, while continuously whipping with a whisk. As butter melts, eggs will cook and thicken sauce. Pour sauce into a stainless steel or ceramic gravy boat. Sprinkle with paprika.

PARCHMENT SEAFOOD
Servings: 4

This is perhaps the most popular parchment paper dish you will find at many seafood restaurants. Serve with fresh rolls and a garden salad.

1 lb. salmon
1 lb. haddock
½ lb. small sea scallops
8 large shrimp, shelled, deveined
1 tbs. olive oil
1 cup corn, fresh or canned (drained)

1 medium carrot, grated
½ cup diced scallions
1 onion, thinly sliced
4 tbs. grated Parmesan cheese
2 tbs. lemon juice
2 tbs. butter

Rinse fish under cold water. Lay out four 18-x-15-inch sheets of parchment paper and fold in half. Unfold paper and brush inside with olive oil. Scatter ⅛ of corn, carrot, scallions, onion and cheese on one side of each sheet. Place ¼ of salmon, haddock, scallops and 2 shrimp over vegetables. Do not overlap seafood. Drizzle with lemon juice. Cover seafood with equal amounts of remaining vegetables and cheese. Dot with butter. Fold and tightly seal each packet. Place packets on baking sheets and bake in a preheated 425° oven for 15 minutes. Transfer packets to individual serving plates, allowing guests to open them at the table.

STRIPED BASS BAKED WITH SALSA

Servings: 4

Also known as rockfish, greenhead or striper, the meat is firm and bright white. Seven to eight shiny black and silver lines from head to tail are a distinguishing feature of this much sought-after saltwater fish.

2 lb. striped bass fillets
1 can (1 lb. 12 oz.) crushed tomatoes
  in puree
3 garlic cloves, minced
1 medium onion, finely chopped

2 tbs. chopped jalapeño pepper
1 tbs. chili powder
½ tsp. finely chopped cilantro
cilantro sprigs for garnish

Rinse fish under cold water and pat dry. To make salsa, in a large bowl combine tomatoes, garlic, onion, pepper, chili powder and cilantro. Mix thoroughly and refrigerate for at least 2 hours. Line a 12-x-12-inch ovenproof casserole with parchment paper. Arrange fish in casserole. Do not let fish overlap. Spread 1 cup of salsa over fish. Bake uncovered casserole in a preheated 400° oven for 20 minutes. Serve fish immediately, garnished with cilantro sprigs. Pour extra salsa into individual ramekins for dipping.

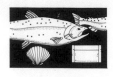

POACHED RED SNAPPER
Servings: 2

You can substitute pike or lake trout for the red snapper.

1 lb. red snapper fillets
2 qt. water
1 onion, sliced
1/4 cup chopped celery
4 thin slices ginger root
2 whole cloves
1/8 tsp. whole coriander
1/8 tsp. dried thyme
2 peppercorns
2 sprigs parsley
1 tsp. vinegar
2 tbs. lemon juice
1 bay leaf

Rinse fish under cold water. Bring water to a boil in a 3-quart sauté pan. Add all ingredients except snapper to water, reduce heat and simmer for 5 minutes. Lay out two 18-x-15-inch sheets of parchment paper and fold in half. Unfold paper and place half of fish on one side of each sheet. Fold paper packets and secure with paper clips for poaching (see page 4). Lower packets into sauté pan and simmer for 5 minutes. Turn packets over and sauté for 5 more minutes. Remove from pan and transfer to individual serving plates. Serve with *Dijon Mustard Sauce*.

DIJON MUSTARD SAUCE

4 tbs. butter
2 tbs. Dijon mustard
1 tsp. chopped fresh parsley

Melt butter in a saucepan over low heat. As butter begins to boil, remove from heat, add mustard and whip to blend. Stir in fresh parsley.

DESSERTS

BAKED BANANAS

Servings: 4

This is a delightful and elegant dessert.

4 ripe, peeled bananas
¼ tbs. lemon juice
1 tbs. butter, melted
¼ cup confectioners' sugar
⅓ cup coarsely grated walnuts

Slice bananas lengthwise into thirds. Combine lemon juice, butter and sugar in a bowl and mix well. Lay out four 10-x-15-inch sheets of parchment paper and fold in half. Unfold paper and place 3 banana slices on one side of each sheet. Pour mixture over bananas and cover with walnuts. Fold and tightly seal each packet. Place packets on a baking sheet in a preheated 375° oven for 15 minutes. Serve on individual serving plates, allowing guests to open their own aromatic desserts.

RICOTTA ROLL UPS
Yields: 64

Parchment paper is perfect for making this delicate but usually messy dessert.

DOUGH

½ lb. margarine

2 cups flour

½ cup ricotta cheese

2 eggs, separated

Combine margarine, flour, cheese and egg yolks. Mix thoroughly to form dough. Separate dough into 8 balls. Place in a plastic bag and refrigerate for 4 hours or overnight. Roll out balls of dough into 6-x-10-inch rectangles. Spread filling evenly on dough, leaving 1-inch border along sides. Starting at wide end, roll up each rectangle of dough and pinch together at seam. Brush tops with egg whites. Place seam side down on a parchment-lined cookie sheet in a preheated oven at 375° for 30 minutes. Cool and cut into ¾-inch slices.

FILLING

2 cups finely chopped walnuts

1 cup sugar

1½ tbs. ricotta cheese

2 tbs. cinnamon

Combine walnuts, sugar, cheese and cinnamon. Mix ingredients thoroughly.

CINNAMON-GRAHAM APPLES

Servings: 4

This is an easy-to-prepare dessert. For a special treat, serve over vanilla ice cream or frozen yogurt.

4 apples
4 graham crackers
½ tsp. cinnamon
4 tsp. lemon juice
2 tbs. butter

Peel, core and slice apples into thin wedges. Crush graham crackers into crumbs. Lay out four 18-x-15-inch sheets of parchment paper or 4 hearts and fold in half. Unfold paper and place ¼ apples on one side of each sheet next to fold. Cover apples with equal amounts of graham cracker crumbs. Sprinkle with cinnamon, drizzle with lemon juice and dot with butter. Fold and seal tightly. Place packets on a baking sheet and bake in a preheated 425° oven for 12 minutes. Transfer packets to individual serving plates, allowing guests to open desserts at the table.

CREAM PUFFS
Yields: 24

These are absolutely heavenly. The French cream filling is the best I've ever had.

PUFFS

½ cup butter
1 cup water
1 cup flour
4 eggs

Combine butter and water in a saucepan. Bring to a boil. Add flour and mix thoroughly. Remove from stove. Add unbeaten eggs 1 at a time, continuously mixing dough. Place teaspoon-size portions of dough on a parchment-lined cookie sheet in a preheated oven at 425° for 10 minutes. Reduce heat to 400° and bake for an additional 30 minutes. Remove from oven and cool on a wire rack.

FRENCH CREAM FILLING

½ pint all-purpose whipping cream
¾ cup milk
1 box (3.4 oz.) instant vanilla pudding
confectioners' sugar

In a large bowl, whip cream until volume is doubled. Do not over beat. In another bowl, mix milk with pudding. Combine cream with milk and pudding. Mix thoroughly. Cut puffs in half. Remove tops and fill hollow centers with cream. Replace tops and refrigerate. Before serving, sprinkle with confectioners' sugar.

TOASTED ALMOND PEARS

Servings: 4

This appetizing blend of delightful ingredients creates a wonderful dessert.

⅛ cup sliced almonds
4 large pears
4 graham crackers

2 tbs. brown sugar
⅛ cup raisins
2 tbs. butter, melted

Lay almonds in a single layer on parchment-lined baking sheet and toast in a preheated 325° oven for 10 minutes. Peel pears, cut in half and remove cores and stems. Slice pears into thin wedges. Crush graham crackers into crumbs. In a small bowl, combine almonds, brown sugar, graham crackers, raisins and butter. Lay out four 18-x-15-inch sheets of parchment paper or 4 hearts and fold in half. Unfold parchment and place ¼ of the pears on one side of each sheet next to fold. Spoon mixture evenly over pears. Fold and tightly seal packets. Place packets on a baking sheet and bake in a preheated 400° oven for 20 minutes. Transfer packets to individual serving plates, allowing guests to open them at the table.

OPULENT PLUMS

Servings: 2

This recipe was chosen for its simplicity as well as its luscious flavor. Cinnamon and cloves add a subtle spicy touch to the fruit.

6 large plums
¼ cup brown sugar
¼ cup chopped walnuts
⅛ tsp. ground cloves
⅛ tsp. ground cinnamon
2 tsp. butter

Slice plums into 4 sections and remove pits. In a small bowl, combine brown sugar, walnuts, cloves and cinnamon. Lay out two 15-x-15-inch sheets of parchment paper or 2 parchment circles and fold in half as on page 3. Divide plum slices equally, placing them on one side of each sheet next to fold. Sprinkle with brown sugar mixture and dot with butter. Fold and tightly seal each packet. Place on a baking sheet and bake in a preheated 425° oven for 12 minutes. Transfer packets to serving plates. Cut open and top with frozen yogurt, if desired.

APPLE PIE
Servings: 8

In this recipe the same sheet of parchment paper is used to roll out the dough, line the pie plate and protect the edges of the pie from burning.

PIE CRUST

2 cups flour
1 tsp. salt

⅔ cup vegetable shortening
7½ tbs. water

Mix flour and salt together in a medium bowl. Use a pastry blender to cut in shortening until the mixture resembles small peas. Drizzle with water and mix with a fork until dough is moistened and can be formed into a ball. Divide dough in half. Roll out dough between a pastry board and a 15-x-15-inch sheet of parchment paper to form two 12-inch circles of dough. Place a 9½-inch pie plate on same parchment paper and trace a circle the size of the bottom of pie plate. Fold paper in half, matching circle lines to form a half circle. Cut out circle, leaving entire section of paper outside circle intact. Reserve this piece for covering edges of pie during baking. Put parchment circle in bottom of pie plate. Place a 12-inch circle of dough in pie plate over parchment circle and set aside.

APPLE FILLING

3 tbs. flour
¾ cup sugar
1 tsp. cinnamon
⅛ tsp. ground nutmeg
3 lb. apples, cored, peeled, sliced
2 tsp. lemon juice
2 tbs. butter

Combine flour, sugar, cinnamon and nutmeg in a small bowl. Place apple slices in a large bowl. Pour mixture over apples and mix. Spoon apples and remains of mixture into formed pie crust. Drizzle with lemon juice and dot with butter. Cover with remaining sheet of dough. Flute edges, cut slits in top and glaze with drops of water. To prevent edges from excessive browning, place the outer section of the parchment circle over pie, creating a border over edges. Crimp and tuck paper under plate. Bake in a preheated 400° oven for 60 minutes. Serve warm.

BAKED BANANAS WITH CHOCOLATE

Servings: 4

This recipe is written for 4 servings but can easily be changed to any amount. It's a simple yet scrumptious dessert.

4 ripe bananas
2 oz. finely grated semi-sweet chocolate squares
1 tbs. finely grated coconut
1 tbs. butter, thinly sliced

Peel and slice bananas in half lengthwise. Lay out four 18-x-15-inch sheets of parchment paper or 4 hearts and fold in half. Unfold papers and lay out 2 banana slices on one side of each sheet. Top bananas with grated chocolate and sprinkle with coconut. Place slivers of butter on top of chocolate and coconut. Fold and tightly seal each packet. Place packets on a baking sheet and bake in a preheated 425° oven for 8 minutes. Transfer packets to individual serving plates, allowing guests to open this delightful dessert at the table.

SECKEL PEARS

Servings: 6

Baked Seckel pears in parchment are absolutely wonderful. My dad introduced me to the unique flavor of this small plump fruit which is naturally spicy and sweet. Sometimes the tastiest recipes are the simplest. Do not substitute any other variety of pear.

6 Seckel pears
1 tsp. sugar
1 cup water

Cut pears in half lengthwise. Cut out stems and remove cores. Lay pear halves, cut side up, on a parchment-lined casserole dish. Fill center of each pear half with water and sprinkle with sugar. Cover casserole with parchment paper. Bake in a preheated 400° oven for 12 minutes.

BLUEBERRY PIE
Servings: 8

Use fresh or thawed frozen blueberries and surprise your family with a pie for dessert. The parchment preparation is explained on page 149 with the crust recipe.

pie crust, page 149
6 cups blueberries
¾ cup sugar
¼ cup flour
½ tsp. ground cinnamon

¼ tsp. ground nutmeg
3 tsp. lemon juice
2 tbs. butter
1 tsp. milk

Prepare a parchment-lined pie plate and rolled out dough for top and bottom crust. Place blueberries in a large bowl. Combine sugar, flour, cinnamon, and nutmeg in a small bowl. Pour mixture over blueberries and mix. Spoon blueberries and remaining mixture into pie plate. Drizzle with lemon juice and dot with butter. Cut remaining rolled-out dough into ½-inch strips. Cover top of pie with strips in a lattice design and flute edges. Brush lattice strips with milk for glaze. Place outer section of parchment circle over pie. Crimp and tuck paper under plate to hold in place. Bake in a preheated 400° oven for 50 minutes. Serve warm.

MICKEY DEE'S FOOLPROOF BROWNIES

Yields: 18

This recipe is a favorite of my mother's. The brownies bake perfectly, won't stick to the bottom of the pan and lift out easily. For the grand finale, add a scoop of vanilla ice cream and hot fudge sauce.

3 oz. unsweetened chocolate
⅓ cup butter or margarine
1 cup sugar
2 eggs, beaten

1 tsp. vanilla
½ cup flour
1¼ cups coarsely chopped walnuts
½ tsp. baking powder

Combine chocolate with butter and melt in a double boiler or microwave. Add sugar to eggs and beat. Combine sugar and eggs with chocolate and butter; add vanilla and mix. In a large bowl, combine flour, walnuts and baking powder. Combine all ingredients and mix until blended. Place an 8-inch square cake pan on a sheet of parchment paper and trace outline of pan onto paper. Cut square out. Line pan with parchment square and pour in batter. Place in a preheated 375° oven and bake for 25 minutes.

BAKED STUFFED APPLES
Servings: 4

This is the perfect conclusion for an elegant meal. Serve with a cup of hazelnut or French vanilla gourmet coffee.

3 tbs. sugar
1/4 cup raisins
1 tbs. chopped almonds
1 tbs. chopped walnuts
1 tbs. chopped pecans
1 tsp. ground cinnamon

1/4 tsp. ground cloves
3 tbs. butter, melted
3/4 tsp. confectioners' sugar
4 medium apples, peeled
1/2 cup white wine

In a small bowl, combine sugar, raisins, almonds, walnuts, pecans, cinnamon and cloves. In another small bowl, combine melted butter with confectioners' sugar. Slice tops off apples and save. Spoon out cores, leaving some apple at bottom. Spoon raisin-nut stuffing into cavities. Top each with 1/4 butter-sugar mixture. Place tops back on apples. Lay out four 15-x-15-inch sheets of parchment paper and place 1 stuffed apple in center of each sheet. Pour 2 tbs. wine over each apple. Join corners of each parchment sheet together to form a bag. Secure closed with metal wire or paper clips. Place bags on a baking sheet and bake in a preheated 375° oven for 45 minutes.

SNOW BALLS

Yields: 12-18

This is a perfect cookie — nutty-flavored, not too sweet, delicate and easy to bake with parchment paper.

2 tbs. margarine
3 tbs. sugar
1 cup flour
1 cup finely chopped walnuts
1 tsp. vanilla
confectioners' sugar

Blend together margarine and sugar. Add flour, walnuts and vanilla. Mix thoroughly. With your hands, roll dough into walnut-sized portions and place on a parchment-lined cookie sheet. Bake in a preheated 350° oven for 15 minutes. Roll in confectioners' sugar while still warm.

ITALIAN CHOCOLATE COOKIES
Yields: 24

This is the perfect accompaniment to a tall cup of cappuccino.

DOUGH

1 cup sugar
1 cup shortening
3 eggs
5 tbs. cocoa
1½ tsp. ground cloves
1½ tsp. ground cinnamon

3 tbs. baking powder
½ cup milk
1 tsp. vanilla
3½ cups flour
1 cup coarsely chopped walnuts
Chocolate Frosting, follows

In a large bowl, mix sugar and shortening with a rubber spatula. Add eggs, cocoa, cloves, cinnamon, baking powder, milk and vanilla. Add flour, ½ cup at a time, mixing well each time. Add walnuts and mix again. Shape into 1-inch balls; place on a parchment-lined cookie sheet and bake in a preheated 350° oven for 15 minutes. Remove from oven and cool cookies on a wire rack. The same parchment paper can be used several times. Ice cookies with *Chocolate Frosting*.

CHOCOLATE FROSTING

2 cups confectioners' sugar
3 tbs. cocoa
1 tsp. vanilla
2-3 tbs. milk
colored sugars for sprinkling

In a medium bowl, combine sugar, cocoa and vanilla. Add milk as needed, starting with 2 tbs., to form thin frosting. For easy cleanup, place cookies back on parchment to frost. Sprinkle with colored sugars.

LEMON COOKIES
Yields: 24

This is a soft cookie with a nice semi-sweet lemon flavor. It's wonderful with a good cup of hot coffee or tea.

½ cup shortening, melted
1 cup sugar
3½ cups flour
7 tsp. baking powder
2 eggs
½ tsp. salt
1 tbs. lemon extract
1 cup milk
Lemon Frosting, follows

In a large bowl, thoroughly combine shortening and sugar. Add remaining ingredients and mix together. Add a little more flour to mixture if it is too sticky. Flour hands and form cookies into ¾-inch balls. Place balls on a parchment-lined cookie sheet and bake in a preheated 400° oven for 10 minutes. Cool on a wire rack before frosting.

LEMON FROSTING

2 cups confectioners' sugar
1 tsp. lemon extract
milk as needed to blend
sifted confectioners' sugar

In a medium bowl, combine sugar and lemon extract. Starting with 2 tbs, add milk as needed to form thin frosting. Using a good quality pastry brush, paint frosting on cookies and sprinkle with sifted sugar.

ANISE BISCOTTI
Yields: 24

You don't have to buy expensive biscotti. It's easy to bake at home yourself. This Italian biscotti makes an ideal accompaniment to a delicious cup of espresso.

2½ cups flour
2 tsp. baking powder
¼ tsp. salt
¼ cup butter

1 cup sugar
3 eggs
1 tbs. anise extract

Sift flour, baking powder and salt. Set aside. With an electric mixer, beat butter with sugar. Add eggs, one at a time, mixing well each time. Add anise extract and mix again. Add flour and beat until completely blended. Cut mixture in half and form into two 10-x-15-inch oval loaves. Place each loaf on a parchment-lined cookie sheet and bake in a preheated 350° oven for 20 minutes. Remove from oven and cool for 5 to 10 minutes on a wire rack. Cut into 1- inch slices. Lay slices on the same parchment-lined cookie sheet and bake for 5 minutes. Turn slices over and bake for 5 additional minutes. Place cookies on wire rack to cool.

BUTTERHORNS

Yields: 64

These have been a traditional holiday family favorite for years. The recipe is from my mother. They're a wonderful treat and always a crowd-pleaser.

2 cups flour
½ cup butter
¾ cup sour cream
1 egg yolk

1 cup sugar
1 tbs. cinnamon
½ cup finely chopped walnuts

Blend together flour and butter. Add sour cream and egg yolk and mix well. Roll into a ball, wrap in parchment paper and refrigerate for 3 hours or overnight. In a small bowl, combine sugar and cinnamon. Cut dough into 8 equal pieces. Roll each piece into a thin circle about 6 inches across. Cut each circle into 8 wedges as if you were cutting a pizza. Sprinkle with cinnamon and sugar. Cover with a thin layer of walnuts. Roll up each piece, starting at the wide end, and pinch to hold together. Place on a parchment-lined cookie sheet in a preheated 375° oven for 20 minutes. This recipe can easily be doubled and you can reuse the parchment paper.

ULTIMATE CHOCOLATE CHIP COOKIES
Yields: 24-30

This traditional recipe works exceptionally well with parchment paper for incredible chocolate chip cookies. No more burnt cookies!

½ cup butter
1⅛ cups flour
½ tsp. baking soda
6 tbs. brown sugar
6 tbs. sugar

½ tsp. vanilla
1 egg
6 oz. semi-sweet chocolate chips
2 oz. finely grated chocolate
½ cup coarsely chopped walnuts

Let butter stand at room temperature for 2 hours. In a small bowl, combine flour with baking soda; mix and set aside. Cream together butter, sugars and vanilla in a large bowl. Add egg and mix well. Add flour, ¼ cup at a time, mixing well each time. Add chocolate chips, grated chocolate and walnuts. Mix thoroughly. Drop rounded teaspoon-size pieces of dough on a parchment-lined cookie sheet. Bake in a preheated 375° oven for 13 minutes. Cool cookies on a wire rack. The parchment paper can be used several times.

ROASTED CHESTNUTS

Servings: 6

To the Italians, CASTAGNE ARRESTITI. When wrapped in parchment paper, the chestnuts never dry out and open easily. There's no need to drizzle with oil or soak in water.

30 medium fresh chestnuts

Wash chestnuts and pat dry. Slash chestnuts on the flat side with a sharp knife. Place a 15-x-15-inch sheet of parchment paper on a baking sheet and fold in half. Unfold paper and lay chestnuts, slash side up, on one side of parchment. Seal tightly with a series of thin folds along sides. Place chestnuts in a preheated 425° oven for 45 minutes. Serve warm.

MAIL ORDER SOURCES FOR PARCHMENT PAPER

Chef's Catalog
3215 Commercial Avenue
Northbrook, IL 60062-1900
1-800-338-3232

Baker's Catalogue
King Arthur Flour
P.O. Box 876
Norwich, VT 05055-0876
1-800-827-6836

Colonial Garden Kitchens
P.O. Box 66
Hanover, PA 17333-0066
1-800-245-1415

Williams-Sonoma
P.O. Box 7456
San Francisco, CA 94120-7456
1-800-541-2233

Taylor Gifts
355 East Conestoga Rd.
P.O. Box 206
Wayne, PA 19087-6677
1-800-647-6677

William Glenn
2651 El Paseo Lane
Town and Country Village
Sacramento, CA 95821
1-800-842-3322

INDEX

SERVE CREATIVE, EASY, NUTRITIOUS MEALS WITH NITTY GRITTY® COOKBOOKS

Cooking with Parchment Paper
The Garlic Cookbook
Flatbreads From Around the World
From Your Ice Cream Maker
Favorite Cookie Recipes, revised
Cappuccino/Espresso: The Book of
  Beverages
Indoor Grilling
Slow Cooking
The Best Pizza is Made at Home
The Well Dressed Potato
Convection Oven Cookery
The Steamer Cookbook
The Pasta Machine Cookbook
The Versatile Rice Cooker
The Dehydrator Cookbook
The Bread Machine Cookbook
The Bread Machine Cookbook II
The Bread Machine Cookbook III

The Bread Machine Cookbook IV
The Bread Machine Cookbook V
Worldwide Sourdoughs From Your
  Bread Machine
Recipes for the Pressure Cooker
The New Blender Book
The Sandwich Maker Cookbook
Waffles
The Coffee Book
The Juicer Book
The Juicer Book II
Bread Baking (traditional), revised
The Kid's Cookbook
No Salt, No Sugar, No Fat
  Cookbook, revised
Cooking for 1 or 2, revised
Quick and Easy Pasta Recipes,
  revised
15-Minute Meals for 1 or 2

The 9x13 Pan Cookbook
Extra-Special Crockery Pot Recipes
Chocolate Cherry Tortes and
  Other Lowfat Delights
Low Fat American Favorites
Now That's Italian!
Fabulous Fiber Cookery
Low Salt, Low Sugar, Low Fat
  Desserts
Healthy Cooking on the Run,
  revised
Healthy Snacks for Kids
Muffins, Nut Breads and More
The Wok
New Ways to Enjoy Chicken
Favorite Seafood Recipes
New International Fondue Cookbook
Authentic Mexican Cooking

Write or call for our free catalog.
BRISTOL PUBLISHING ENTERPRISES, INC.
P.O. Box 1737, San Leandro, CA 94577
(800) 346-4889; in California (510) 895-4461